Elections, Leadership, and National Development in Nigeria

Practices, Problems, and Prospects

Chima Imoh (PhD, Public Policy and Leadership)

Heritage Publishing Company

Houston, United States of America

i

Heritage Publishing Company,
7447 Harwin Drive,
Houston, TX 77036.

Library of Congress Control Number: 2014913942

Imoh, Chima

Elections, Leadership, and National Development in Nigeria/Chima Imoh

P.cm.-(elections, leadership, and development)

ISBN-978-0985479237

1. Elections-Leadership practices- development.
2. Electoral competition- political leadership performance- National Development. I. Title. II. Series

Printed in the United States of America

PREFACE

This book is about elections, political leadership performance, and national development in Nigeria. Although democracy is becoming the prevalent and acceptable form of governance in such Sub-Saharan African countries as Nigeria, there is need to understand the domestic dynamics under which electoral competition influences the quality of leadership and national development.

The major purpose of the book is to explore and explain the circumstances under which elections play crucial roles in the job performance of elected political elites and its effects on the development of Nigeria. There are obvious linkages between the basic political values of a democratic state and the leadership performances of elected officials, as well as its national development. The effects of the interactions of unethical political behaviour and sluggish improvements of the already poor national development are evident in Nigeria.

Nigeria is bestowed with enormous natural and human resources; and hence, has the potential for technological and economic advancement. The country also has the potential to create and sustain self-reliance and advancement in major spheres of human development. Efforts at meaningful developments have, however, failed to yield the desired results due to poor leadership. This failure at national leadership becomes more challenging when considerations are given to the fact that the natural resources of Nigeria, which contribute about 80% of the Gross Domestic Product (GDP), are controlled by the national government.

In comparison with other African and Asian countries, Nigeria at its independence, had dynamic public institutions, competent professionals, and a vibrant civil society; and was considered the "phoenix of African hopes"[1]. Contrary to expectations, Nigeria has remained a nation-state, which by all democratic and leadership criteria, performs poorly in comparison with similar nation-states in Sub-Sahara Africa[2].

Although the colonial legacies constitute part of Nigeria's political and developmental problems, it still remains unfortunate that, unlike Malaysia, Indonesia, and India with similar legacies, Nigeria has been unable to formulate policies that promote national integration and effective leadership. The problem of economic underdevelopment in Nigeria is, therefore, more complex than the effects of such exogenous factors as colonialism.

Obviously, the authoritarian military regimes, which interrupted elected democratic regimes through coups d'état, have impeded the political development processes. Even the so-called democratic regimes have been simply electoral dictatorships that combined regular elections with a number of democratic deficits; such as corruption, poor systems of checks and balances on the executive and ineffective legislative branch of government[3]. These civilian regimes have used the conduct of multiparty elections to mask the prevalent authoritarian domination, plagued by election-rigging, abuse of power, and widespread corruption[4].

The low levels of electoral competition in the political system of Nigeria have had adverse effects on the quality of leadership, as well as the development of the nation. Genuine electoral competitions create and guarantee accountability; serve as constraints on executive arbitrariness; and improve representation and participation. These in turn, create a balance between the politician who is supposed to supply good governance and the citizens who demand good governance.

The weak public institutions and the lack of transparency and accountability of political office-holders in Nigeria immensely contribute to pervasiveness of maladministration and poor governance. It is imperative that without the leadership to foster genuine electoral practices, the quality of governance in Nigeria will remain poor, stalling the development of the country.

Essentially, the absence of genuine democratic culture, lack of national vision, weak political and unethical leadership has undermined Nigeria's development[5]. Fundamentally, Nigeria's political system has a strong executive, but weak law-and-order institutions. Moreover, corrupt bureaucracies have made addressing Nigeria's leadership and development problems more challenging.

In Nigeria, most of the opportunities for advancement in life are controlled by the state; and it could, therefore, be very challenging to get the political office-holders to adhere to the rules of democracy and civilized decency. To gain or hold onto power, the Nigeria politician would stuff the ballot boxes, steal votes, buy electoral officials, harass, intimidate the opposition, and even murder political rivals. Electoral officials are bribed to falsify the vote counts; returning and announcing unbelievable and implausible results. The overall political landscape of Nigeria is still bestridden by electoral fraud, corruption, and domination of the state apparatus by the ruling party.

In my doctorate dissertation research, I determined and explained how the conducts of genuine free and fair elections have positive relationships to public safety and rule of law, protection of human rights, effectiveness of governance, control of corruption, and human development. There are, therefore, obvious positive relationships among the improvements in levels of electoral competition, the quality of political leadership, and national development in

Nigeria. This book therefore seeks to propagate that genuine electoral practices will influence the quality of political leadership; thus engineering improvements in the development of Nigeria.

Another purpose of this book is to shed some light on the Nigeria's development problems; especially, those that arise from the absence of genuine elections and the attendant adverse effects on the quality of political leadership. This is because, economic factors, adverse world market, non-participation in the global supply chain, and deficit internal structures do not adequately explain the poor developmental performance of Nigeria; such domestic issues as quality of internal political institutions and leadership also play decisive roles. Nigeria has its own unique development problems that are contingent on some internal political factors.

As this book will explain, efficient and functioning political institutions create good governance that contributes to transparency and accountability in government operations.

My hope is that this book will serve as a useful source of complimentary reading and knowledge for public policy practitioners, civil rights organizations, incumbent and opposition political parties; international donors, and elections monitoring organizations.

Chima Imoh, PhD.

ABOUT THE AUTHOR

Dr Chima Imoh has a degree in Geodetic
Engineering and a master's degree in international
management. He has a doctorate degree in Public
policy and Administration, specializing in public
management and leadership. Dr Imoh is a member
of the National Honor Society for Public Affairs
and Administration, United States of America.
The author has lectured and worked in public
institutions in the United States and in Africa. Dr
Chima Imoh is the author of two books, *Cultural
Competence for Global Management* and
*Policymaking and Development Strategies for
Local Governments in Nigeria*. He is also a co-
author of the book, *Competency for Public
Administration,* edited by Dr Susan T. Gooden
and Dr Kris Major.

CONTENTS

Introduction

Historical Perspectives

Nigeria is in the western part of Africa around what is geographically known as the Gulf of Guinea, which borders the country to the south. The republic of Benin is to the west and the republic of Cameroon is to the east. Niger Republic is north and the Chad Republic borders the northeast. Nigeria has a population of about 150 million and occupies an area of 920,000 square kilometers, slightly more than twice the state of California[1].

Historical records indicate that the colonization of Africa obtained "formal approval" at the Berlin conference of 1984/85[2]. The British government colonized the more than 250 ethno-cultural groups in Nigeria; and administered the country under the northern and southern protectorates. These protectorates were later amalgamated into one administrative entity. This forceful colonization of Nigeria came with the imposition of alien systems and conditions. These included the imposition of the European culture and the nation state system, forceful incorporation of contending and hostile ethnic groups/kingdoms into one state, destruction of indigenous checks and balances, and the introduction of authoritarian political regimes[3].

For the maximization of their own interests, the colonizing powers ruled Nigeria with absolute authoritarianism. Hence, the colonial powers sowed the first seeds of authoritarianism into the political structure of Nigeria. This authoritarian leadership model, has, unfortunately, remained and has continued to contribute to the inhibition of democratic and leadership development in Nigeria. The past and current development woes of Nigeria, therefore, emanate partially from the failure of its colonial and postcolonial leaders to establish the prerequisite democratic leadership elements that are essential for national development[4].

Moreover, the development model used by the departing colonial powers, which; emphasized government control of resources, minimized functions of the market and encouraged state ownership of productive resources was not discarded; but was continued after independence. Rather than developing its own pathway to economic development, Nigeria continued to maintain the neo-colonial-dependent economy[5]. Thus, Nigeria continued the economic prescriptions of the former colonial powers, producing primary crop with the primary purpose of feeding the industrial base of Great Britain. Before the discovery of oils reserves, therefore, Nigeria had focused on investing in agriculture, producing industrial raw materials for export trade to European industries.

Further, the departing colonizing powers, using the theoretical underpinning of modernization, which espoused that more capital investment leads to growth, encouraged the newly independent nation to mobilize investment resources for accelerating growth without giving consideration for the existence of such other prerequisites for development as leadership[6]. Ever since Nigeria attained independence from the British Empire in

October 1st, 1960, therefore, poor leadership has bestridden her political landscape.

Although a new civilian regime was ushered in Nigeria in 1999, this move from outright authoritarianism has not transformed into democratic regimes as was popularly thought; but has rather transformed into regimes that combine democratic and non-democratic characteristics. The political system and leadership in the country is still characterized by corruption, poorly working systems of checks and balances between the executive and legislative branches of government. The electoral processes of Nigeria are tainted by manipulations, abuse of state power, the harassment of opposition candidates, and election rigging. Obviously, Nigeria's existing governing system with strong executive, central revenue control system, weak law and order institutions, and dysfunctional and corrupt bureaucracy makes it difficult to address Nigeria's development problems.

PART I

Political Systems

Chapter 1

The Political Systems of Governance

Political systems of governance occupy a theoretical spectrum that range from autocracy to democracy. In between these political leadership models are authoritarianism and electoral authoritarianism, otherwise called incoherent or restricted democracy.

Autocracy

Fully institutionalized autocracies restrict citizen participation. Usually, the selection of chief executives is through hereditary or defined rules of succession from established political elites[1]. They do not, therefore, hold competitive elections. Moreover, the chief executives exercise power without meaningful checks from the legislature, judiciary, or civil society, and institutions[2]. However, just below these fully institutionalized autocracies are those that share their characteristics, except that they share some power with elected officials[3].

Authoritarianism

Any modern day autocratic governance which is characterized either by the authoritarian rules of personalized leadership, military dictatorship, or one-party dominance[4] could be regarded as authoritarianism. These less institutionalized autocracies could have rules of succession that are less-clearly defined, but allow some level of political participation or limits on executive authority[5].

As Theodore Vestal had indicates in *Ethiopia: A Post-Cold War African State,* authoritarianism characterizes a political system in which highly concentrated and centralized power structures are used to maintain political power through repressive systems that exclude potential challengers and opposition[6]. The Canadian political psychologist Robert 'Bob' Altemeyer had, in *The Authoritarian Specter*, also argued that the authoritarian system constitutes a value syndrome that comprises of submission to authority, and authoritarian aggression[7] and is therefore an anti-thesis to democratic ideals. In authoritarian regimes, elections are not conducted, and when conducted, are usually facades in which electoral competition is in reality eliminated[8], and in some cases the opposition vanquished both physically and structurally.

Under this system, non-elected officials make political decisions; the bureaucracy operates independent of rules, and elected officials show no concerns for the constituencies that they serve[9]. Moreover, in outright authoritarian regimes, real legislatures do not exist, and when they do, are so much in the firm control of the ruling executive or party machinery that no real checks and balances exist between the executive and legislatures[10], and are therefore essentially one-party states. Such states become, in reality and practice, one-party systems; structured by the weakening of the civil society, with no guarantees made for civil liberties or tolerance for meaningful opposition[11]. Another main problem with authoritarian regimes is the difficulty in depersonalizing political authority, which is the prerequisite for the rule of law and separation of powers among the legislature, judiciary, and executive arm of government[12].

In authoritarian systems, the absence of institutionalized and recurring methods of selecting political leaderships creates uncertainties[13]. Authoritarianism is therefore, a regime in which the alternation of power is neither institutionalized nor recurring[14]. Authoritarianism should, therefore, be seen as institutionalized dictatorship that is either absolute one-man rule or where the set pattern for political advancement and leadership does not yield to electoral competition.

Democracies

There are multiple definitions of democracy. The 19th century Austrian-American economist and political scientist Joseph Alois Schumpeter had in, *Capitalism, Socialism and Democracy,* emphasized a minimalist and procedural version of democracy as "that institutional arrangement for arriving at political decisions in which individuals acquire the power to decide by means of competitive struggle for the people's votes"[15]. In the same procedural perspectives, Seymour Martin Lipset in *Political Man: The Social Bases on Politics,* defined democracy as a "political system which supplies regular constitutional opportunities for changing government officials[16]. Also, Samuel Huntington (1984, 195) in, *The Third Wave: Democratization in the Late 20th Century,* defined democracy as a political system in which its "most powerful collective decision-makers are selected through periodic elections in which candidates freely compete for votes and in which virtually all the adult population is eligible to vote[17].

Democracy starts with the citizens; with the pillars of the democratic framework embedded in the rights of the citizens and the ability of the state to guarantee equal rights of the citizens through constitutional and legal processes[18]. Generally, most democratic principles encourage representation, basic rights, and the sovereignty of the people. The concept of democracy hinges on the proposition that political power emanates and rests with the citizens[19]. The French historian Alexis de Tocqueville had, in his 1835 landmark book, *Democracy in America,* indicated that the very essence of democratic government consists of the absolute sovereignty of the majority; with the legislature being the embodiment of this absolute power and supremacy[20].

Democracy has become an attractive form of governance because its principles embrace human needs and desires and can, in reality, often deliver them[21]. The key elements of democratic practices are the separation of power, independence of the judiciary, institutionalized checks and balances, participation, competition, and regular free and fair elections. The main attributes of the requirement of free and fair elections are participation, competition, and fairness. It is, therefore, noteworthy that greater checks on politicians and greater accountability to citizens are both indicators by which a distinction can be made between democratic regimes from electoral authoritarian regimes[22].

Chapter 2

Democracy: Classical Theories and Constructs

Democracy has widely become regarded and largely accepted as the ideal system of government that provides the political and social structure within which we can live happy and fulfilled lives under the protection of the government. A strong democracy is operationally definable as one in which political participation is fully competitive, the executive recruitment is elective, and the constraints on the executive are substantial[1]. Generally, most democratic principles encourage representation, basic rights, and the sovereignty of the people as the concept is fundamentally hinged on the proposition that political sovereignty originates with the citizens[2].

Democratic governance involves free debates and legislative procedures, which are subject to public scrutiny and criticism[3]. Democracy has, therefore, increasingly become the only basis of legitimate government; and the idea has caught on that regime is legitimate only when it is based on the will of the people[4].

The practical definition of democracy can also be approached from either the procedural or conceptual perspectives. The procedural perspectives of democracy seek to derive a descriptive definition from the characteristic features that existing democratic governments have in common; whereas the conceptual definitions seek to derive from the history of liberal and democratic thought, focusing on the values that are integral to ideas of liberal democratic governance[5].

The renowned American political scientist, Robert Dahl (1915-2014) had, in *A Preface to Democratic Theory*, emphasized that there is no democratic theory; rather, that there are democratic theories[6]. Democratic theories, hence, come in different shapes and sizes, and there is, by no means, no consensus on which strand is preferable[7]. Within its theoretical frameworks, democracy could, however, be analyzed from the perspective of three theories of competition, egalitarianism, and deliberation.

The Competitive Theorists

The theory of competitive democracy, initiated by the 19th century Austrian-American economist and political scientist Joseph Alois Schumpeter (1947) had an economic perspective to democracy as a free competition for free votes in the political realm. Schumpeter had, in the book, *Capitalism, Socialism and Democracy*, surmised that from this free market-style orientation, forms of anticompetitive behaviors are expected, and tolerable in democracies[8]. According to this perspective, the free market-style of competition is necessary, and promoting the perfection of the competition is not necessary for the democratic system. This school of thought postulates that the protection and preservation of the integrity of ballot system is of more importance to the democratic system than the promotion of competition[9]. The deductive reasoning of this perspective is that a democratic system cannot be genuine if the voting system is compromised[10], and protecting the votes of the citizens rather than promoting the enabling environment for free and fair competitions among contending parties is paramount. The integrity of the ballot system is, therefore, an integral aspect of creating a genuinely competitive electoral system.

Egalitarian Theorists

The egalitarian theorists led by Robert Dahl had, in the book, *Democracy and its Critics,* argued that democracy is not about the realization of majority will through democratic accountability and representation; but rather about a pluralist society in which a multitude of minorities seek to advance their goals through both electoral and non-electoral means[11]. This school of thought insists that the essence of democracy should be the promotion and protection of fundamental rights and the enthronement of an egalitarian society. In this book, Robert Dahl placed more emphasis on basic rights as the substantive core of procedural democracy.

The value of democracy lies, therefore, not in representation, but in the protection of rights, namely, the ability to hold officials accountable or throw them out of office[12]. The core of the argument is that the "democratic measure" of a society is represented by such parameters as protection of basic human rights, supremacy of the people's sovereignty, and its egalitarianism.

The Deliberative Theorists

Deliberative democracy stresses the creation of practices that encourage and promote collaboration between citizens and government; focusing on free and open political discussions and deliberations[13]. The proponents of deliberative democracy believe that any doubts of the ability of citizens to participate in democratic deliberation are in themselves, doubts of democracy itself[14].

The deliberative democrats offer a multiple of reasons for their claim of the superiority of this perspective. They posit that, in a democratic system in which citizens are politically equal and are bound to disagree, deliberative democracy demands that each citizen should be able to explain whatever he or she believes[15]. Moreover, because the process would require that citizens who deliberate provide justifications for their stance, the qualities of debates become enhanced[16]. This is because the deliberative exchanges lead participants to correct flaws in their analysis, and can also make them move from fixated positions and explore new alternatives that had been unknown to them[17].

Chapter 3

Democracy: Contemporary Theories and Constructs

Essentially, the contemporary constructs of democracy has such complementary systems as "polyarchy", hyper democracy, and direct democracy and also such conceptual and practical anti-theses as electoral authoritarianism.

Robert Dahl's theory of 'polyarchy"

Polyarchy refers to a system in which a small group rules; and mass participation and decision-making are confined to choosing leaders in elections managed by competing elites[1]. The concept is an outgrowth of the elitism theories that developed in the early 20th century to counter the classic definition of democracy as the power or rule of the people[2]. Robert Dahl had coined 'polyarchy' to describe this unique representative government, which seems somewhat utopian[3].

The characteristics of 'polyarchy' are a system in which control over policy-making decisions are constitutionally vested in elected officials, and citizens have an effectively enforced rights to freedom of expression, particularly political expression, including criticism of the officials and conduct of the government. In terms of political participation, citizens in a 'polyarchy', have enforceable rights of forming and joining associations and interest groups who could exercise the rights to influence the government in so far such is done through peaceful means[4]. In the book, *A Preface to Democratic Theory,* Robert Dahl, argued that when it comes to building collective decisions, each person in a political community is entitled to be given equal consideration to his or her interests[5]. In *Polyarchy*, Robert Dahl also argued that for the effectiveness of this representative democracy, the two requirements of ensuring political controls by the citizens are electoral participation and competition[6].

A "polyarchy" has also been described as a set of institutions and procedures that are meant to ensure that effective political decision-makers are chosen in fair and free elections[7]. The system has been further characterized the conditions for free and fair elections as having access to independent information, citizens' ability to express their opinions freely, join parties and organizations without fear of institutionalized retaliation[8]. Essentially, a "polyarchy" is a nation-state that has designed the procedures and necessary conditions for meeting these democratic principles[9].

Hyper Democracy

Hyper democracy is a political dream in which, all the characteristics in a democratic regime do not only exist, but are also close to perfection[10]. Although the scope and scale of democracy would be enhanced by polyarchy, it is still possible to make democracy more inclusive or more egalitarian[11]. The argument here is that all citizens should express their views directly and equally; and if for any reasons representatives must be selected, tossing a die is preferable to ballots[12].

In a classic article titled 'Democracy before Democracy' and published in, *International Political Science,* Yves Schemeil argued that the free competition and free deliberation associated with this system are expected to lead to rational consensus; and the subsequent unanimous decisions would often be the outcome of strong belief in common sense truth that bypasses political cleavages[13]. This is one democratic perspective that seems quite utopian because creating free competition and free deliberation in the affairs of humans seems totally unrealistic.

Direct Democracy

As Bernard Manin had argued in *The Principles of Representative Government,* direct democracy is a form of government that enables the citizens to override representative democracy and directly make their voices heard[14.] Direct democracy remains a method for people to access government and influence the political process directly[15]. Robert Rotberg also argued in, *Governance and Leadership in Africa, that* direct democracy creates accountability in public institutions, while at the same time maintaining the vitality of community life[16]. The controversial nature of this form of democracy is so profound that some have argued that the direct involvement of citizens that excludes representation is not workable and could have consequences that would have adverse effects on the long-term health of the democracy[17]. Obviously, given the size, and diversity of the modern nation-state, direct citizen participation is not a feasible expectation[18].

Direct democracy was once considered in the United States as the option of protecting the people away for the chokehold of party bosses and the party machineries that limited the individual's to exercise liberty and personal happiness[19]. In the United States, citizen initiatives and referenda have become the manifestations of direct democracy, and have been designed to grant the citizens direct access to policymaking.

Restricted democracies (Electoral authoritarianism)

In between the authoritarianism and democracies are electoral authoritarianism (restricted democracies) that are neither authoritarianism nor democracies; but they rather combine an incoherent mix of authoritarian and democratic practices[20]. Electoral authoritarian regimes are political systems that combine regular democratic elections with a number of democratic deficits, such as corruption, lack of press freedom, and poorly working systems of checks and balances between the executive, and legislative branches of government[21]. In these regimes the existence of e such democratic practices as multiparty elections tend to blur the reality of authoritarian domination[22]. A political system descends into electoral authoritarianism when the violations of democratic ideals become so serious as to create an uneven playing field between incumbent government and the opposition parties[23].

Chapter 4

Concepts of Genuine Democracy

The pillars of the democratic framework are embedded in the rights of the citizens and the ability of the state to guarantee equal rights of the citizens through constitutional and legal processes[1]. Democracies will have institutionalized processes for open, competitive, and political participation, choosing and replacing chief executives in open, competitive elections[2].

The Polity IV Project of the *center of Systemic Peace,* which shows the trends, political regime characteristics, and transitions of the major countries of the world, is invaluable when considering level of democracy in a country. The project, which was initiated by Ted Robert Gurr in the 1970s, has evolved over years, largely due to the work done by Monty Marshall and Keith Jaggers; who conceive democracy as three essential interdependent elements; (i) the presence of institutions and procedures through which citizens can express preferences about alternative policies and leaders, (ii) the existence of institutionalized constraints on the exercise of power by the executive, (iii) the guarantee of civil liberties to all citizens in their daily lives and acts of political participation[3]. The arising practices of rule of law, checks and balances, freedom of press and other aspects of democracy are manifestations of these three broad principles[4].

Larry Diamond[5], in *The Spirit of Democracy* had also outlined the attributes of democracy as having:

(i) Substantial individual freedom of belief, opinion, speech, publication, broadcast, assembly, demonstration, and petition.

(ii) The freedom of ethnic, religious, racial, minority groups, and even the historically excluded majority groups to practice their religion and culture, as well as participate equally in political and social life.

(iii) The right of all adult citizens to vote and be voted for, as long they meet the age and competency requirements.

(iv) Genuinely open and competitive elections.

(v) Legal equality of all citizens under a rule of law, in which the laws are clear, publicly known, universal, and not retroactive.

(vi) Independent judiciary that neutrally and consistently applies the law; protecting individual and group rights

(vii) The due process of law and freedom of individual from torture, unjustified detention, or interference in their personal lives by the state.

(viii) Institutional checks on the power of elected officials, by independent legislature, court systems, and other autonomous agencies.

(ix) A vibrant press and "civil society" that ensures pluralism in sources of information

(x) Institutional control of the military and state security apparatus by civilians who are ultimately accountable to the people through elections.

The democratic ideal in itself seeks to guarantee equality and basic freedom; the empowerment of the citizens, resolution of disagreement through peaceful means, and to enthrone political, social, and renewals without disruption[6]. The practice of democracy also offers popular control over the elected leaders, equal rights and liberties, political freedom, freedom from wants, upholding the rule of law, justice, and security[7].

Democracy, therefore, means more than regular conduct of elections. A genuine democracy must be able to deliver what the people expect in terms of development and decent governance[8]. Democracy must also provide ongoing means for achieving accountability and responsiveness, as well as making political leadership broadly representative[9].

Essentially, a stable democratic state would have competitive elections, whose outcomes are uncertain; as well as potentialities for alternation of parties in power. At the minimal level, the people should be able to elect or replace their political leaders through regular, free, and fair elections[10]. The hallmark of a genuine democracy is, therefore, the ability to resolve the problems of leadership succession by means of elections without turmoil[11].

Democracy as an important component of free government, however, carries certain risks, which, if not checked, could enthrone domination[12]. Such risks include the absence of genuine electoral competition, which, for instance, transformed most of the civilian regimes in Nigeria into electoral dictatorships. The conduct of elections does not mean that they are free and fair[13]. For that reason, free and fair contested elections can be used as the procedural definition of democracy. As Robert Dahl indicated in *Political Opposition in Western democracies,* such concepts as freedom of speech, freedom of association, and free and fair elections are some of the central components of democracy[14].

Elections are 'free' when the "legal barriers to entry into the political arena are low; when the competing candidates, parties, and their supporters are free to campaign, and when people can vote for whom they want without fear and intimidation"[15].

Elections are 'fair' when, among other criteria; they are "administered by a neutral authority; there are specific precautions against fraud; law enforcement agencies treat competing candidates and parties impartially; independent monitoring of voting and counting is allowed; and the electoral processes and procedures are widely known, transparent and impartial[16]. Elections, therefore, serve to express the collective will of the people, going further to consolidate democracy only when the voting and the electoral processes and procedures are free and fair[17].

Elections that deviate from these standards of "free" and "fair" can only serve the different ends that manifest into autocracy or electoral authoritarianism[18]. Democracy is of low quality or is an electoral authoritarianism when there are serious abuses of human rights, significant constraints on personal freedom, discrimination against minorities, a weak rule of law, compromised judiciary, rampant corruption, state domination of mass media, and unresponsive government[19]. The United Nations, in resolution 16/163 recognized that states are responsible for ensuring free and fair elections that do not tamper with vote counts[20].

Genuine electoral competition provides avenues for imposing political costs on elected officials who act in ways that are beneficial to their private interests and at the expense of the public interest. This political accountability, therefore, places constraints and sanctions on the behavior of public officials. These sanctions are further enhanced as the quality of electoral competition increases. For instance, improvements in the electoral competition would increase the likelihood that alternative parties will expose the corruption of the incumbent government.

Although, Nigeria has a multiparty electoral system, has significant opposition, and has some space for the civil society and dissenting intellectualism; elections are, however, riddled with fraud. Electoral competition is so constrained and dominated by the domineering power of incumbency that it is difficult to call the system a democracy. Nigeria, therefore, occupies the ambiguous space between democracy and overt authoritarianism, and is therefore classifiable as an electoral authoritarianism.

Democracy has not yielded the desired benefits to Nigeria largely because the outcome has always been electoral authoritarianism. Genuine transition entails, not just from authoritarian to the democratic system of governance; but also the consolidation of the democracy. Samuel Huntington had, in *The Third Wave: Democratization in the Late 20th Century,* argued that the consolidation of democracy occurs only after two electoral turnovers, with the party in power at the beginning of the transition losing a subsequent election, turning over power to the opposition, and the new incumbents losing power to another party in a subsequent election[21]. Electoral turnovers will obviously assist in the consolidation of democracy in Nigeria.

Chapter 5
Sovereignty of the People:
The core of Democratic Governance

In their classical article published in *Democratization,* titled, "How To Construct A Database Of Liberal Democratic Performance," and widely used by political and social scientists to conceptualize democracy, Joe Foweraker and Roman Krznaric indicated that the core values of liberal democratic governance hinge on the key principles of liberty and equality; manifesting as the rule of law and sovereignty of the people[1]. They argued that the rule of law, practiced through the legal values of civil, property, political, and minority rights, in turn, guarantees individual freedoms, and protections. They also argued that on its part, the sovereignty of the people is practiced through such institutional values as accountability, representation, constraints on executive, and participation.

The measure of democratization, should therefore, be based on such indices as basic human rights, supremacy of the people's sovereignty and its egalitarianism. A state or regime is, hence, not democratic by calling it so or by merely embracing such institutions of democracy as legislature and judiciary, as is the case in quasi-democracies or electoral authoritarianism[2]. The value of democracy does not only rest on representation, but also in the protection of rights; namely, the ability to hold officials accountable or throw them out of office. One key mechanism for enforcing this accountability is through the periodic conduct of genuine elections.

Being democratic also means welcoming the existence of opposition parties, and letting them organize and campaign freely against the ruling party. Robert Rotberg had, in *Governance and Leadership in Africa* argued that under genuine democratic systems, opposition parties thrive, elections are free and fair, and ruling parties are sometimes voted out of power[3]. More so, the democratic state holds regular elections, supervised by independent and impartial electoral commissions[4]. A democratic state espouses and supports such essential as freedoms of expression, worship, movement, assembly, and from want[5].

In a democratic state, the sovereignty of the people is upheld, encouraged, and nurtured by creating the right environments for political accountability to the citizens, political participation of the citizens, protecting the political rights of the citizens, and genuine electoral competition among political contenders. The article 21 of the Universal Declaration of human rights (UDHR) stipulates that political authority should be based on the sovereignty of the people[6]. Ultimately, the government is responsible to the people, and political office holders should be controlled by the people through elections.

Political accountability to the citizens

Democracy offers the advantage of rooting public policies in political accountability[7]. This political accountability ensures the responsiveness and accountability of the government to the governed; the transparency of government actions and services; and the accessibility of all to government programs and services;

and all these should be of primary concern in a democratic state.

Also, by generating public accountability, democracies impose checks on elected officials and policy makers[8]. The public demand for accountability creates incentives for governments to adopt policies that are conducive to growth[9]. Moreover, by compelling elected officials to consider the electoral consequences of the behavior, political accountability increases the chances of delivering public goods[10].

Another source of political accountability is the level at which existing democratic structures possess real opportunities for alternation of power. This alternation of political power is better assured by the presence of credible opposition. The presence of credible opposition guarantees that there is an alternate government capable and waiting to take over from the incumbent government. This in turn, puts pressure on the ruling government to be responsive and accountable to the citizens.

Protecting Citizens' political rights

As the egalitarian theorists led by Robert Dahl had argued, democracy could rather be about a pluralist society in which a multitude of minorities seek to advance their goals through both electoral and non-electoral means[11]. These egalitarian theorists place more emphasis on basic rights; arguing that the value of democracy lies largely on the protection of the political rights of the citizens; namely, the ability to hold officials accountable or throw them out of office[12].

Political Participation of citizens

A key element of democracy is its ability to empower the citizens. Empowering the citizens entails their active participation through their ability to elect or dismiss their political leaders by means of genuine competitive elections. A robust and healthy democracy is only as possible as the active participation of the citizens in public life[13]. Effective participation requires that citizen would be able to form their own political associations and pressure groups[14].

If, however, the people are to participate in politics, they would need to have some confidence that their individual participation would contribute or make some difference to governance[15]. Article 25 of the International Covenant on Civil and Political Rights (ICCPR) indicates that citizen participation in the public affairs of the state, especially in genuine periodic elections, is fundamental to democracy[16].

A series of positions regarding the relevance of direct citizens' participation to the values of democracy and the effectiveness of the policymaking process have been canvassed. As Jean Jacques Rousseau (1712-1778) had argued, the health of a polity depends on active citizen participation and involvement in all aspects of governance[17]. In a democratic society, citizens have a fundamental right to participate[18] as citizenship participation is the cornerstone of democracy[19]. Citizen participation is important for a variety of reasons: to promote democracy, build trust, increase transparency, enhance accountability, build social capital, reduce conflict, ascertain priorities, promote legitimacy, and cultivate understanding, or advance fairness, and justice[20].

Essentially, democracy requires some degree of citizen participation in governance; as it helps to protect the rights of the electoral minority as well as the racial minorities.

Direct participation even becomes more relevant to the extent that it has the ability to extend effective power to the disadvantaged groups in such ways that enhance and protect their rights. Obviously, a degree of equality in political participation is symbolically important for a legitimate political system[21], as some minimal level of it is necessary to maintain stability in a political community[22]. Evidently, the key to political development is an electorate that is both willing and able to participate in domestic politics[23].

Autocratic and democratic regimes both regulate participation; but from different perspectives and means. Autocratic regimes do so by using a single channel of participation-such as one party- that imposes limits on dissent; whereas democratic regimes allow nonviolent competition of opinions and influence[24]. Democratic rule essentially rests on the accountability of elected officials to the citizens, as well as the entitlement of citizens to participate in the government directly or through representation.

Political participation, when enhanced through more democratic competition, becomes an essential component of democracy, guaranteeing such liberty that no groups could subject others to their whims and caprices[25]. The democratic framework, therefore, helps citizens to participate by debating and resolving their value differences as to reflect consensual views that approximate closely to public interests; thereby reducing political conflicts.

The renowned social and political theorist, Philips Pettit had, in *Republicanism: A theory of Freedom and Government,* argued that a modern state that desires to minimize domination through democratic competition must not only make political engagement desirable but must also deliver tangible products[26]. The state, therefore, not only has to be non-dominating but also has to track the interest of the citizenry[27]. To achieve this, political and state institutions must make it possible for the citizenry to effectively participate. Encouraging all citizens to participate in the political process reduces political domination. A political good that is, therefore, necessary in Nigeria is enabling the citizens to participate freely and fully in the democratic process.

Genuine Electoral Competition

In the book, *Democracy and Development,* Adam Przeworski, Michael Alvarez, Jose Cheibub, and Fernando Limongi posited that democracy is the system of governance where government offices are filled through contested elections[28]. The defining characteristic of democracy is the regime where high political offices and legislature are chosen through contested elections in which the political competition is organized in such a manner the outcomes are reasonably uncertain. A democratic state would always hold regular elections, supervised by independent and impartial electoral commissions; as the repeated conducts of genuine competitive elections produces improvements in civil liberties and strengthens civic organizations by giving officeholders some incentive to service[29].

As Robert Dahl and the other egalitarian theorists had argued, organized competition and elections, through the power of the vote, validate the basic concept of modern democracy[30]. The integrity of the ballot box as the expressed will of the people should be a fundamental interest of the state in the way of preserving its integrity or preventing its corruption. A democratic system cannot, therefore, be considered genuine if the ballot is compromised, or preferences are coerced[31]. To fulfill the fundamental rights to vote or be elected as specified in article 25 of the International Covenant on Civil and Political Rights (ICCPR), the state is required to conduct genuine and periodic elections[32]. Elections are genuine when they are competitive; the will of the voters freely expressed; and votes are counted honestly and accurately.

The theory of democracy emphasizes that competition between political parties creates and fosters more responsive governance by shepherding elected leaders toward service and accountability. Enduring democratic systems are hence, characterized by meaningful political participation and peaceful competition[33]. To achieve this, the state and political processes must make it possible for the citizenry to effectively participate in genuine electoral competitions. Electoral competitions in Nigeria have, however, not always attained the levels desirable for elevating the leaders toward the higher ideals of service and accountability.

PART II

Leading a Nation:
Forms and Concepts of Political Leadership

Chapter 6

The Spectrum of Political Leadership: authoritarian to democratic Leadership

Leadership is a form of power in which the wielders compete with others, using the resources available to them to influence others toward the attainment of set goals[1]. Leadership is, however, dependent on the performance system and environment within which leadership occurs[2]. Leaders must adapt to the environment because the phenomenon of leadership comes with the need to achieve the goals desired by the stakeholders. Leadership is, therefore, situational, and the concepts that define leadership are culturally and environmental-specific. Although leadership involves that use of power, the exercise of power itself is not leadership[3].

Power is not the act of changing the attitude and behavior of others, but rather the potential to do so[4]. When used, power may either be deployed either toward uplifting or toward domination. The exercise of power is, however, a mutual influence between the leader and the follower. Although one party may be more dependent than the other, a relationship exists when each party has something of value to offer to the other[5]. Interdependence, therefore, exists between the parties; with the individuals over whom power is exercised having a counter-power. A leader may exercise the power to work for the enhancement of the well-being of the followers; the followers do exercise a measure of control through the counter-power that arises from their ability to work more productively or less, which would, in turn, have either a positive or negative effect on the leader's job performance evaluation. It is this counter power that should put pressure on leaders to use their power judiciously and for the well-being of the followers.

Although countries have mixed features of openness, competitiveness, and regulation, the core attributes of democracy and autocracy define the opposite ends of a leadership spectrum[6]. As Robert Tannenbaum and Warren Schmidt indicated in their 1958 classical work, *"How to Choose a Leadership Pattern,"* the continuum of political leadership extends from autocratic leadership to democratic leadership[7]. These authors had argued that democratic leadership, which allows followers to function with set institutionalized limits, occupies one end of the spectrum; whereas autocratic leadership, which does not entertain inputs from followers, occupies the opposite end. A political leadership could, therefore, be autocratic, authoritarian, or democratic.

Autocratic Leadership

Autocratic leadership occurs through hereditary or rules of succession from established political elites[8]. They do not, therefore, hold competitive elections for the selection of chief executives. These chief executives often, exercise power without meaningful checks from the legislature, judiciary, or civil society, and institutions[9]. As indicated earlier in this book, modern day autocratic governance, characterized by rules of personalized leadership, military dictatorship, or one-party dominance[10] is, however, authoritarianism.

Authoritarian Leadership

Authoritarian leadership operates under rules of succession that are less-clearly defined; even though it allows some level of political participation or limits on executive authority[11]. Under an authoritarian leadership, elections are not always conducted, and when conducted, are usually facades in which electoral competition is in reality eliminated[12], and in some cases, the opposition is vanquished both physically and structurally. Although authoritarian leadership styles vary in their political institutions and civic freedoms, what they have in common is that the authority to rule is not allocated through competitive elections[13].

Another problem with authoritarian leadership is the difficulty in depersonalizing political authority, which is the prerequisite for rule of law and separation of powers among the legislature, judiciary and the executive arms of government[14]. An authoritarianism leadership should, therefore, be regarded as institutionalized dictatorship that is either absolute one-man rule or a political system in which the set pattern for political leadership and advancement does not yield to electoral competition.

Authoritarian leaders are usually conservative and not always willing to accept or adapt to changing circumstances and new ideas[15]. This need for the authoritarian leader to protect the past as well as inhibit constructive changes propels a culture the leans toward incompetence.

The authoritarian leader makes every effort to dominate while expecting unquestionable obedience from disciples. To the authoritarian leader, power flows from the top (and not from the people), and relationships are based on domination, dependence, and obedience. Authoritarian leadership is, however, sustainable not only through subordinates who control the system, but also by the docile public that is unwilling or unable to rebel against the control[16]. Authoritarian leaderships tend to thrive on coercive power, and must, therefore, be resisted because of its inherent tendencies toward destruction[17].

Democratic Leadership

Democratic and authoritarian leadership models are distinct and contrasting forms of governance, with the principal differences being on the acquisition and transfer of executive power[18]. Another fundamental difference is on the exercise of political power as authoritarian leaders are usually dictators, neither elected nor voted for by the people[19]. More so democratic leaders give followers freedom to initiate and operate, whereas the authoritarian leaders impose their wills on followers using authoritative forces to motivate followers[20]. Democratic leaders are usually willing to adapt to changing circumstances and new ideas. Rather than suppress dissent, democratic leaders use it as creative forces to greater effectiveness and more competence[21]. Usually, the more developed a democratic state is, the more it is most likely to sustain democracy.

Electoral authoritarian Leadership

In between the authoritarian and democratic leadership styles is electoral authoritarian leadership that operates under a system that combines mixes of authoritarian and democratic leadership[22]. This leadership style is always plagued by such authoritarian characteristics of frequent human rights abuses, utter disregard for civil liberties and widespread corruption[23].

Under this form of leadership elections are regularly held and bitterly contested[24], but are often rigged to favor the incumbent leadership which wields the instruments of the state. The electoral processes under such leadership are always tainted by manipulations, abuse of state power, and harassment of opposition candidates as is the case with Nigeria's political leadership.

PART III

Nigeria: Problems with
Democratic and Leadership Practices

Chapter 7

Problems of Democratic Practices in Nigeria

The deficits of Nigeria's democracy include the non-accountability of elected officials, disregard for the rule of law, violations of human rights, and election malpractices. Judged by its key elements, democracy in Nigeria falls short of acceptable standards. The reasons for the low standards of democracy could be many, but suffice the discussion of four fundamental problems that include; the perversion of democracy, poor democratic culture, fraudulent electoral practices, and the passivity of the electorates.

Perversion of Democracy: Nigeria's Electoral authoritarianism

At the end of military dictatorship in 1999, although Nigeria moved from outright authoritarianism, it has not transformed into a democracy as is popularly thought; but rather transformed into electoral authoritarian regimes that combine democratic and non-democratic characteristics[1]. Steven Levitsky and Lucan Way had in *Competitive Authoritarianism: The Emergence and Dynamics of Hybrid Regimes in the Post-Cold War Era* described an electoral authoritarian regime as a political system that combines regular democratic elections with such number of democratic deficits as corruption; and poorly working systems of checks and balances between the executive and legislative branches of government[2].

Although the civilian regimes in Nigeria were set up under formal democratic institutions as multiparty elections; these regimes in reality, only mask their authoritarian domination, plagued by frequent human rights abuses, disrespect for civil liberties and widespread corruption. Elections are regularly held, but are often bitterly contested and often rigged to favour the incumbent governments, which, control and wield the inherent powers of the state. The electoral processes have remained tainted by manipulations, abuse of state power, and the harassment of opposition candidates; and therefore, with little or no electoral competition.

When the characteristics of authoritarianism are mingled with regular conduct of elections, the resulting political system is nothing but electoral authoritarianism. The so-called democracy in Nigeria is, therefore, nothing but electoral authoritarianism.

Obviously, the essence of even the minimalist form of democracy is the presence of regular, competitive, and multiparty elections that are largely free and fair[3]. As Ian Shapiro argued in *The Moral Foundation of Politics,* competition is the "life of democracy" and "meaningful political competition requires that there be opposition parties, waiting in the wings, criticizing the government and offering voters potential alternative"[4].

Electoral authoritarianism should, therefore, be seen as institutionalized dictator that is either absolute one-man rule or where the set pattern for political advancement and leadership does not yield themselves to genuine electoral competition. These practices go against the grains of democracy constructs, which are usually attentive to the system through which people compete for votes.

Poor 'democratic culture'

Most societies have certain types of values, beliefs, and customs that shape how their people think and act politically[5]. There is, however, a human propensity to corner power and monopolize available resources which usually leads to conflicts[6]. Nigeria has for a long time, acquired and nurtured a poor 'democratic culture'. These are the resultant effects of a combination of the traditional culture, colonization, and long years of military rules.

First, the traditional culture of the main ethnic groups, namely; Hausa-Fulani, Igbo, and Yoruba are divergent in relation to the core principles of democracy. Following the jihad of the early 19th century, the Fulani Othman Danfodio Empire established dominion over the indigenous Hausa States and appointed Emirs as political heads. The resulting seven Hausa-Fulani emirates had centralized, hierarchical, and rigidly stratified political systems[7].

The Yoruba groups had confederate political systems consisting of multiple quasi-feudal systems with semi-autonomous chiefdoms that had considerable influence over the decisions of such central authorities as the Alaafin of the Oyo Empire and Alake of Egbaland[8].

The Ibo groups, on the other hand, were radically different as they constituted themselves in acephalous or autonomous societies without central authorities, lacking hierarchical political structures[9]. Except for the Onitsha and Oguta people, the effective political unit among the Ibo groups was the village or kindred; with disputes between the units settled by negotiation and compromise[10]. Among the indigenous groups in Nigeria, therefore, the

38

Ibo ethnic group traditionally lived in political structures that had the attributes closest to republicanism.

Obviously, European nations once had feudal political systems too. Whereas, the European feudal systems were, however, swept away when republicanism swept through Europe in the 16th century, the colonizing power in Nigeria retained the feudal unit in a system of rule called indirect rule. In creating the political frameworks prior to independence, the colonizers used the so-called indirect rule to accommodate feudalism alongside modern democratic frameworks. This gave rise to what could be termed as "neo-feudalism". The colonizers even went further to impose this system of neo-feudalism on the Ibo groups by creating the "warrant chiefs" system that was obviously alien to the Ibo culture.

Worse still, colonial governance in Nigeria was in the form of an authoritarian administrative apparatus with a powerful and power-wielding governor at the helm of affairs[11]. To be able to extract and maximize their own interests, the colonizing powers ruled Nigeria with absolute authoritarianism, thereby, exacerbating the already existing traditional authoritarian cultures. This forceful colonization of Nigeria with the authoritarian imposition of alien systems and conditions contributed to the overall poor 'democratic culture' in the society.

The long years of military dictatorship, however, contributed largely to the prevailing poor "democratic altitude" of the Nigerian citizenry. The political climate of Nigeria has, therefore, for a long time, been marred by the existence of authoritarian and pseudo-democratic regimes[12]. This authoritarian leadership model, has, unfortunately, remained and has continued to contribute to the inhibition of democratic and leadership development in Nigeria.

Obviously, when a people cultivate and nurture a democratic culture, they begin to value democracy as the best form of government; realizing and affirming the basic human rights of the citizens; and the rights to vote and participate in the political life of the country[13]. This is because a democratic culture provides peaceful means to manage, resolve, or accommodate deep political differences[14]. A democratic culture would, therefore, embrace moderation, accommodation, cooperation and bargaining with the opposition[15].

Fraudulent Electoral practices

A government is not democratic just because its leaders are civilians; but because the road to power and the existing political institutions and the processes of governance are in accord with the working concepts of democracy[16]. Such working concepts of democracy would include free and fair elections, especially the protection of the integrity of the ballot box.

Unfortunately, the electoral processes in Nigeria have remained marred by manipulations, abuse of state power, the harassment of opposition candidates, and election rigging. For instance, presidential elections are often rigged to favor the incumbent presidents as they wield the instruments of the state[17]. The stakes become even higher in re-elections, when, in order to return the presidents to power, the rigging becomes more extensive[18]. Regrettably, elections in Nigeria only represent the interest of the incumbent political elites rather than the will of the people.

Essentially, in Nigeria, incumbent presidents,

governors, and other political office holders manipulate elections to remain in office despite their inept governance, poor economic and infrastructure development, low standard of living, and charges of corruption[19]. The incumbent officials, especially the governors and presidents would rather devise more dubious means to hijack the electoral processes than improve their governance. The critical issue is the absence of free and fair elections, with the elected officials, therefore, not dependent on the electorate to win elections. Specifically, elected presidents, governors, and officials in Nigeria perform poorly and yet the citizens are unable to vote them out because they manipulate the electoral processes through extensive rigging, using the coercive machineries of the state to impose the fraud on the citizens[20].

The absurdity of Nigeria's political situation is that, although, the people are completely dissatisfied with the performances of the governments, the same dissatisfied people are purported to have continually, at each election cycle, renewed the mandates of the inept governments. These political leaders therefore make the people inconsequential to their stay in power; thereby subduing the need for accountability and good leadership. The electoral process in Nigeria is, therefore, highly questionable and fraudulent[21].

Obviously, elections in Nigeria are not "contested elections" because there are usually no uncertainties as to the outcomes. Losing the influence of their votes, and hence no influence over election outcomes, the entire citizenry becomes largely disadvantaged. Democracy is therefore impelled, and loses its value as the stability of the democratic system depends on the effectiveness and legitimacy of the political system.

Passivity of the Electorates

The Nigerian electorates are outstandingly passive to the usurpation of their sovereignty. In voting for elected officials, citizens merely yield their sovereignty to such official only on temporarily basis. Such sovereignty is transferred through the electoral ballots and should never be usurped under any circumstances. The Nigerian electorate, however, watches in docility as the politicians forcefully and falsely declare themselves elected in utter disregard of the expressed electoral wishes of the citizens.

A sustainable democratic culture requires that citizens are respectful of government authority but yet, are watchful of it abuses. Democracies work best when they provide electoral choice, potential for alternation of power, checks on the ruling elites, avenues for exposure and punishments for abuse of power, and legal and political avenues for redressing grievances[18]. These can only be achieved by the reactive and engaged, and not passive electorates.

Using Indicators of Democracy to Compare Nigeria with some other African Countries

Using the 'Polity score' of the Polity IV Project; an internationally recognized parameter for determining the level of democratic practices in nations, the quality of electoral practices in Nigeria will be compared with some other African countries. The "polity Score" captures the authority spectrum of regimes on a 21-point scale that ranges from −10 (full autocracy, with no elections) to + 10 (consolidated democracy with genuine electoral competition).

The spectrum spans from fully institutionalized autocracies in which there are no elections; through incoherent authority regimes, in which electoral malpractices are prevalent; to fully institutionalized democracies in which there are genuine electoral competitions.

The polity IV project examines the concomitant qualities of democratic and autocratic authority in governance with a dataset that covers all major independent states of 163 countries over the period1800-2014.

Using the Polity score, a comparison of Nigeria's level of democratic practices with some countries in Africa over the years 2000 to 2013, and is shown on table 1.

Table 1

Countries	Annual Polity Scores													
	2000	2001	2002	2003	2004	2005	2006	2007	2008	2009	2010	2011	2012	2013
Mauritius	10	10	10	10	10	10	10	10	10	10	10	10	10	10
S. Africa	9	9	9	9	9	9	9	9	9	9	9	9	9	9
Botswana	8	8	8	8	8	8	8	8	8	8	8	8	8	8
Ghana	2	6	6	6	8	8	8	8	8	8	8	8	8	8
Nigeria	4	4	4	4	4	4	4	4	4	4	4	4	4	4
Kenya	-2	-2	8	8	8	8	8	7	7	7	8	8	8	9
Benin	6	6	6	6	6	6	7	7	7	7	7	7	7	7
Zambia	1	5	5	5	5	5	5	5	7	7	7	7	7	7

The polity IV project has a three-point categorization: (i) Polity Score: -10 to -6 as autocracies or authoritarianism.

The institutionalized autocracies (-10 polity score) restrict citizen participation. Usually, chief executives are selected through hereditary or defined rules of succession from established political elites[22]. However, modern day autocratic governance has become characterized by the authoritarian rules of personality-cult leaders, or one-party domination[23]. These are less institutionalized autocracies that have less clearly defined rules of succession, while allowing some level of political participation or limits on executive authority[24].

(ii) Polity Score: -5 to +5 as electoral authoritarianism or restricted democracies.

The countries with polity scores of -5 to + 5 are in between the autocracies and democracies, and are neither autocracies nor democracies, but rather combine an incoherent mix of autocratic and democratic practices[25]. In these regimes, called anocracies, governments hold elections for a legislature that exercises little or no control on the executive, nor allow transparency on political competition among some groups while restricting others[26]. Anocracies can further be classified into closed anocracies (polity score of -5 to 0), and open anocracies (polity score +1 to +5)[27]. From the polity IV index, Nigeria is an open anocracy, restricted democracy, or electoral authoritarianism.

(iii)Polity Score: +6 to + 10 as democracies.

In contrast, the countries with polity score +6 to +10 are considered as consolidated democracies. Some of them have institutionalize procedures for open, competitive, and deliberative political participation, choosing and replacing chief executives in open, competitive elections, imposing structural checks and balances on the power of the chief executive[28].

Graph 1

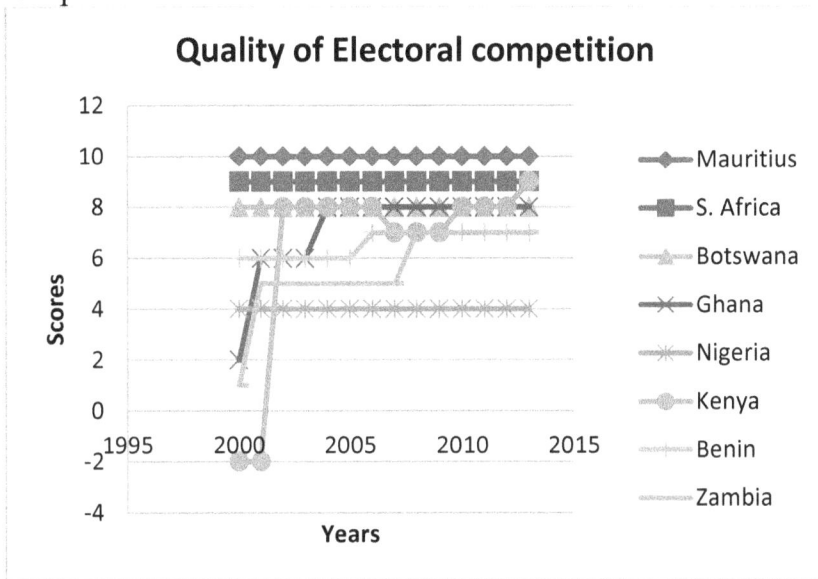

A complete examination of the Polity IV annual, Cross- national, time-series data shows that Mauritius shares the same 'perfect' Polity score of '10' with such western countries as United States, Canada, United Kingdom, Germany, Australia, Switzerland, Norway, Sweden, Finland, Netherlands; and such non-western countries as Japan, Uruguay, and Chile[29].

South Africa shares the same value of Polity score of '9' with India, whereas Ghana and Botswana share the polity score of '8' with Brazil, South Korea, Mexico, Philippines, Indonesia and Argentina.

Nigeria, at polity score of '4' shares such poor performance with Ivory Coast and Zimbabwe; and trails behind other countries with polity score value of '5' as Congo-Kinshasa, Papua New Guinea, Mozambique; as well as trailing Namibia at a polity score value of '6'.

Graph1, showing the 'Polity Scores' of some African

45

countries gives a clearer picture of their levels of democratic practices in comparison with Nigeria.

As can be clearly observed from the graph 1, every of these other African countries are either at the 7-score mark or above, excepting Nigeria at an abysmally low 4-score mark. With the 'polity score' of 4, Nigeria is designated as an electoral authoritarianism. This low score is the result of Nigeria's electoral system with its manipulations, abuse of state power, the harassment of opposition candidates, and election rigging.

Chapter 8

Nigeria's Political Leadership Problems

In a democracy, the power that belongs to the people is bestowed on elected officials on the condition that it is used for the benefit of the people. Nigeria has, however, experienced some good deal of the usurpation of the sovereignty of the people through authoritarian regimes in form of military regimes that have interrupted democratic regimes through coups d'etat that include the 1966, and 1983 coups against civilian governments.

Nigeria has therefore, had more than its own fair share of despotic rulers, who, rather than using power for public goods, use it as an end in itself. These despotic leaders had behaved as if they are law unto themselves. These authoritarian leaders essentially used coercive power to enforce obedience and reward unquestionable obedience even when the subordinate is incompetent. Under the leadership of these despots, infrastructures fell into despair; while healthcare, educational standards and life expectancy have declined.

Unfortunately, however, these civilian regimes in Nigeria have remained plagued by the same authoritarian characteristics as frequent human rights abuses, disregard for civil liberties and widespread corruption. Obviously, the incessant violation of human rights alienates the people from the democratic process[1].

Following nearly 16 years of post-1983 military, a peaceful transition ushered in civilian rule in 1999; with a milestone in April 2007 marking the first civilian-to-civilian but same-party transfer of power in the country.

In Nigeria, political authority is not only essentially centralized, but also has a constitutionally entrenched presidential authority. The wielding of this political authority is, however, largely dependent on self-serving practices that has led to nothing but conflicts and political instability.

As the success or failure of a nation also depends on the political will and determination of its leadership, the poor political leadership performance arising largely from poor political structures and practices are, therefore, much to blame for much of the disappointing economic performances of developmental strategies in the Nigeria. Further, these prevailing leadership practices are also to blame for the failures of the state as the agents of development[2].

The antidote to this political opportunism is to force the elected officials to internalize the cost of this behavior by making governments accountable to the citizenry through competitive elections that allow free and fair contestations[3].

The problems of political leadership in Nigeria can be summarized as arising from: (i) personalized political authority, (ii) prebendalism, (iii) political clientism and abuse of power, (iv) political coercion, (v) obsession with imagined threats to power, (vi) fixation on election rigging, (vii) weakening the institutional checks and balances, (viii) intimidating and weakening the judiciary, and (ix) unbridled corruption.

Personalized Political Authority

The Nigerian political leadership practice is highly personalized. This personalized political authority is indicative of a 'neopatrimonial state' in which there are weak checks on the private appropriation of public resources[4]. A 'neopatrimonial state' indicates a political state in which patrimonial practices co-exist with modern bureaucracy[5]. The "neopatrimonial" nature of governance that exists in Nigeria is characterized by personalized political authority that usually leads to the private appropriation of public resources.

This highly personalize governance style pervades the Nigerian political landscape; converting the people into clients of the rulers rather than citizens whose sovereignty the ruler exercises. Evidence abounds to show that most Nigerian presidents and state governors use public resources as personal slush funds to maintain political dominance and unconditional support from their political cronies. This personalized political authority with its weak checks on the private appropriation of public resources, constitute a major bane of national development, as well as the reason for the failure of the state as an agent of development.

Prebendalism

The term, 'prebendalism', has been used to describe the sense of entitlement of Nigerian public officials and political actors to the revenue of the state. The fundamental purpose of the prebendal governance system is to produce personal resources for those who hold or have access to political power[6]. In such prebendal governance systems as in Nigeria, state offices are sought and utilized for the personal benefits of the seekers and those of their cronies who usually expect and demand their share of the 'booty'.

The public officials feel and demand the rights to share in the resources and revenues accruing to the governments. Essentially, Nigerian political leaders seek public offices as means to accumulate private wealth. The wanton conversion of public wealth to private wealth, therefore, engenders a culture of corruption, poor performances, lack of accountability; making responsiveness irrelevant.

This prebendal governance system, therefore, compromises or abandons such public goods that improve human capital as well as generate such public goods as roads, bridges, markets, education, healthcare, clean water, and effective legal system[7]. Contracts are awarded, not on the basis of who can deliver the best service for the lowest price, but rather to who pays the largest and most assured bribe.

Budgets are not focused toward the projects that would produce the most public goods, but rather on the projects that would produce the most bribes. Government payrolls are over bloated with phantom workers otherwise called 'ghost workers.' Essentially, the scarce public resources that would have being used for such public goods as roads, bridges, markets, irrigation, education, healthcare, public sanitation, and clean water are diverted into private pockets.

Political Clientism and Abuse of Power

The political authority system is largely run on "political clientelism" that includes predatory patronages, prebendalism, and private-enrichment dispositions. Public officials usually appropriate public resources for their own uses. The most disheartening practice is that appointments to public offices are considered as personal grants from higher authorities, and the beneficiaries expected to exploit the "rent" potentials embedded in the office. In turn, the beneficiaries reciprocate through complete loyalty to the benefactors, as well as partake in the sharing of the ill-gotten wealth. The roles of the higher authorities become the creation of the enabling environments for their stooges to usurp and hold onto power; most times by unleashing a reign of terror on political opponents, as well as the bribery of the electoral officers. The protruding situation becomes that social and economic advancement become dependent on relationship to political power rather than the effective use of economic resources.

Political coercion

Most political leaders in Nigeria are self-seeking, using their power to control their followers or subordinates. They are usually self-seeking leaders, more concerned about their own authority and power, and tend to demand unquestioned obedience from subservient subordinates[8]. They are essentially authoritarian leaders who use coercive power to enforce and reward obedience.

As authoritarian leaders, Nigerian political leaders find it extremely difficult to depersonalize political authority. They rather make every effort at dominating; while expecting unquestionable obedience from disciples. To them, power flows from the top, and relationships are based on the acceptance of the domination, dependence, and obedience.

Obsession with Real and Imagined threats to power

In countries where the political institutions are strong,

the political structures for power transfer are usually inviolable. In contrast, in such countries as Nigeria, where the political institutions are weak, political office-holders are usually obsessed with imagine threats to their power. A characteristic of Nigeria's political leadership, therefore, is that political office-holders are more concerned with real or imagined threats to their holds on power than the pursuit of public good and national development.

For such reasons, opposition parties are treated as enemies of the state rather than as component parts of a viable democracy. The opposition parties are therefore, systematically disadvantaged; and with the citizens thus denied the power of checking government behaviors, the quality of leadership is compromised.

Obviously, such governments which are unduly concerned with threats to their holds on power often have shorter developmental horizon and are often preoccupied with appeasing the specific groups that are pivotal to their survival[9]. This feeling of political insecurity is one reason that the various governments in Nigerian always jettison the development prospects of their constituencies in favor of self-survival.

Fixation on election rigging

The two components of democratic competition are participation, and electoral competition. Enduring democratic systems are characterized by meaningful political participation and peaceful competition[10]. The key concepts of democracy are, therefore, meant to ensure, among others, the integrity of this electoral competition[11].

Unfortunately, the political leadership in Nigeria is, however, always fixated on rigging elections rather than embarking on welfare-enhancing programs as means of winning elections. Nigerian political leaders see public offices as avenues for accumulating personal wealth; hence, elections are hotly contested, rigged and manipulated especially by incumbent governments.

Most incumbent governments in Nigeria would rather devise more dubious means to hijack the electoral processes than improve their governance. Hence, political leaders in Nigeria perform poorly and yet the citizens are unable to vote them out because they manipulate the electoral processes through extensive rigging, the use of the coercive machineries of the state, bribery of election officials[12].

Weakening the legislative checks and Balances

Although the legislatures in Nigeria are designed to function as potential platforms for opposition, the executive strives to weaken the legislature. Elections are, therefore, held for a legislature that does not exercise effective oversight and control on the executive.

The legislative arm of government serves, not as a check on the executive, but essentially as an extended arm for corruption, abuse of power, and appropriation of public funds, leading to more centralization of power and authority on the presidency. This weakening of the legislative institutions, the political insecurity, and the centralization and arbitrary exercise of power is characteristic of the pervading neopatrimonial form of governance[13].

Intimidating and Weakening the Judiciary

Almost consistently, political regimes in Nigeria have always adhered to a weak form of rule of law, in which governments regularly attempt to subordinate the judiciary, and at times intimidate the judicial arm of governance. Often this is done by means of bribery, extortion, and in some cases by dismissing judges. More often, there is the tendency for the Supreme Court to function, not as arbiters for constitutionality and legal principles but as advocates of the incumbent regime.

Unbridled Corruption

Transparency International, the world-acclaimed organization on level of corruption within nations, describes corruption as the 'abuse of entrusted power for private gain[14]. Corruption is more prevalent and acutely felt in such less developed countries as Nigeria where political institutions are weak and more vulnerable; and official procedures and safeguards less robust and less transparent. The general effect is that a major portion of the scarce public fund and resources is diverted into private pockets, thereby exacerbating the poverty among the people.

Nigeria, for all intents and purposes, is essentially saddled with poor and malevolent leadership, manned by kleptocrats[15]. The much-needed public funds for these socioeconomic infrastructures are constantly and systematically siphoned and hidden in local and foreign bank accounts[16]. By syphoning the scarce resources that could be used to improve infrastructure, bolster the education systems, and strengthen public health, corruption stifles development[17]. Corruption has eroded Nigeria from the inside out, sickening the justice system until there is no justice to be found; poisoning the police forces until their presence has become a source of insecurity rather than comfort. In the end, the main essence of governance, which is, protecting the people and promoting their common welfare, has become imperiled.

Using Governance Indicators to compare Nigeria with some other African Countries

The level of political leadership performance in Nigeria could be assesses using the World Banks's Worldwide governance Index. The worldwide governance indicators, developed by Daniel Kaufmann, Aart Kraay, and Massimo Mastruzzi for the World Bank Policy department[18]. The data reflects the view on governance from public sector, private sector and NGO experts as the Global Competitiveness Report (World Economic Forum), World Poll (Institute for management Development), the European bank for Reconstruction, African Development Bank, Asian Development Bank, and the United States Department of State[19].

The project provides a meaningful cross-country comparison taken from 35 data sources provided by 33 different organizations. The project reports on the aggregate and individual governance dimensions indicators for 212 countries over the period 1996-2013 for the six dimensions of leadership. The worldwide governance indicators measure six governance indicators: (a) voice and accountability, (b) political stability and absence of violence, (c) government effectiveness, (d) regulatory quality, (e) rule of law, and (d) control of corruption[20].

Table 2 compares the political leadership performance in Nigeria with some other countries in Sub-Saharan Africa, using the World Bank's World Governance Index (WGI) as the leadership indicator for each country. It is noteworthy to indicate that the data for 2001 were unavailable, and were, therefore imputed through linear interpolation.

Table 2

Country	Aggregated World Governance Indicator												
	2000	2001	2002	2003	2004	2005	2006	2007	2008	2009	2010	2011	2012
Mauritius	4.25	4.31	4.30	4.65	4.25	4.32	4.11	4.32	4.85	4.67	4.62	4.90	5.01
S. Africa	2.27	2.14	2.02	2.23	2.50	2.47	2.59	2.08	1.181	1.55	1.51	1.59	1.19
Botswana	3.95	3.93	3.92	5.21	4.43	4.71	3.94	4.05	4.16	3.90	3.99	4.07	4.34
Ghana	-0.58	-0.89	-1.21	-0.44	-0.72	-0.35	0.39	0.47	0.20	0.53	0.60	0.72	0.44
Nigeria	-6.04	-6.77	-7.51	-7.34	-7.46	-6.66	-6.68	-6.76	-6.24	-6.89	-7.03	-6.77	-6.82
Kenya	-4.72	-4.72	-4.73	-4.14	-3.70	-4.24	-3.77	-4.11	-4.51	-4.64	-3.94	-4.19	-4.41
Benin	-0.15	-0.69	-1.22	-1.02	-1.56	-2.30	-1.30	-1.29	-1.41	-1.52	-1.83	-1.80	-2.10
Zambia	-3.05	-3.23	3.47	-2.80	-2.80	-3.34	-2.61	-2.22	-1.82	-2.08	-2.16	-1.72	-1.24

The graph 2 shows the relationship among the governance indicators of these countries; and, therefore, gives a clearer picture of the comparison of their levels of political leadership performance with that of Nigeria.

Graph 2

Leadership Performance Using WGI

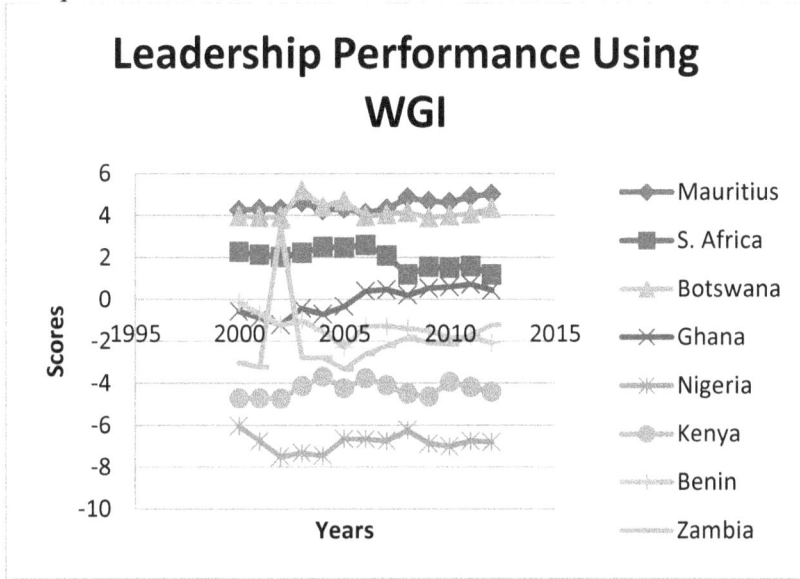

From graph 2, Nigeria lags behind all the other countries as it stays at the bottom of the graph in the quality of leadership performance.

Another comparison of political leadership in Nigeria with some other countries in Sub-Saharan Africa could be made using the Ibrahim Index of African Governance (IAG). This index on African leadership assesses governance against 84 criteria. These criteria, divided in four broad groups, include the public safety and rule of law; participation and human rights; sustainable economic opportunity and human development[21]. These are further broken down to such issues as personal safety, property rights, accountability, corruption, national security, civil rights, and gender equality. Other issues include rural investment, infrastructure development, obtaining licenses, immunization, poverty, health, and education issues.

The comparison is shown on table 3.

Table 3

Country	African Index of Leadership					
	2007	2008	2009	2010	2011	2012
Mauritius	79.0	81.8	82.3	83.3	82.6	82.9
S. Africa	71.7	71.5	71.0	71.3	71.5	71.3
Botswana	75.4	75.5	76.0	76.8	77.4	77.6
Ghana	64.1	64.4	65.6	66.3	67.0	66.8
Nigeria	43.2	43.0	43.2	43.9	43.2	43.4
Kenya	53.5	54.2	51.0	53.2	53.7	53.6
Benin	59.3	57.5	59.1	59.9	59.6	58.7
Zambia	56.1	55.4	56.0	56.8	58.0	59.6

Graph 3 shows relationship among the IAG of these countries and gives a clearer picture of their political leadership performance; with Nigeria also at the bottom.

Graph 3

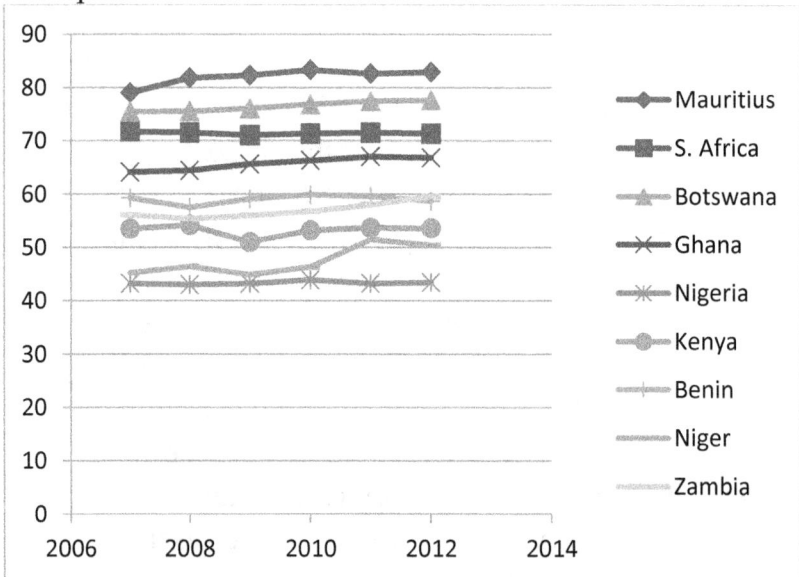

Chapter 9

Nigeria: A Predatory Political System?

The Nigerian political system can also be described as predatory. The predatory political system is such a governance structure in which power is used to control or restrict political and economic competition so that access to economic and political opportunities are primarily available for the benefit of a small group of political allies rather than for public good[1]. In a predatory political system, there is no shared commitment to public good and largely no respect for laws[2]. Political behavior is opportunistic and those that capture political power seek to monopolize and extract the rents that flow from it[3].

Under this system, political leaders do not usually ally on the basis of values and shared visions, but rather on the basis of savoring power and the privileges that flow therefrom. In the predatory Nigerian system, public officials feed on the state and the powerful prey on the nation and weak amongst them[4]. The rich citizens become rich but not through engagements in productive activities, but rather by manipulating political power and privileges, stealing and embezzling from the state or by violating the law[5].

The state becomes the principal instrument of personal advancement and wealth[6]. Corruption becomes the norm as citizens get accustomed to bribing officials even in routine matters as getting or renewing a driving license or getting a tax payment certificate. Corruption ultimately becomes 'widely regarded as a norm' rather than a crime, while the ordinary citizens 'feel powerless, exploited and unhappy'[7].

Arising from the unhappiness, the ordinary citizens who are trapped at the lowest rungs of the socio-economic ladders of the predatory society distrust each other[8]. The distrust, reinforced by ethnic and linguistic differences leads to suspicion rather than collaboration among the oppressed[9]. More often, the predatory elites even mobilize and use the ethnic tensions to divert public frustration of their political failures, misdeeds and exploitation toward the other ethnic groups[10]. This usually leads to religious and ethnic conflicts.

Granted that the predatory state may seem stable if the ruling elites use part of their 'booty" to bribe a small band of the political and business elites or using it to enforce, and maintain political order, such situations do not generate sustainable development[11]. The time horizons become extremely short as no one has confidence in the state and its future[12]. This predatory leadership leads to decline in the political and administrative institutions of the state. This state of affairs manifests in the prevalence of political violence, bureaucratic incompetence and corruption[13]. A self-reinforcing political decadence and economic deterioration sets in; parallel economic activities flourish outside state control; feeding on bureaucratic corruption and shirking of regulations and tax evasion[14].

Larry Diamond[15], in *The Spirit of Democracy*, enumerated the characteristics of a predatory political

system as a society where:
(i) Political elites will use any means and break any rules to acquire power and wealth.
(ii) Politicians bribe electoral officials, beat up or assassinate opposing candidates.
(iii) Presidents silence criticism or opposition by legal manipulation, arrest or even murder.
 (iv) Ministers worry first about the size of their bribe money before considering whether the contracts are of any public value and good.
 (v) Legislators collect bribes to vote for bills.
(vi) Policemen extort rather than defend the public, making the line between the police and the criminal very thin, when it exists.
(vi) Judges do not decide the law impartially, and without fear of favor.
(vii) Custom officials do not inspect goods but rather collect tolls.
(viii) Bankers do not invest but only engage in usury
(ix) Borrowers do not repay.
(X) Contracts are not enforced. Every transaction is twisted to immediate advantage.

Does this describe the Nigerian society? Unfortunately, the characteristics enumerated above aptly describe the Nigerian state. The more predatory the Nigerian system has been becoming, the more the governance is based on the persons rather than on laws and institutions. National decay is setting in. The decay of the predatory Nigeria state manifests in enormous and unbridled corruption; abuse of power and arbitrary use authority; deterioration of public services and common good; and the absence of the enabling environment for economic growth. The challenge and difficulty of sustaining democracy in Nigeria becomes tougher because democracy requires respect for the constitution and laws of the land including the laws against bribery and corruption.

Fortunately, the Nigeria predatory system can be overcome as societies that have overcome predatory political systems have essentially been able to tame the abuse of power; to open up access to political and economic opportunities; and have streamlined the political leadership to impersonal and impartial rules and institutions.

PART IV

Developing the Nation: Politics and Problems of National Development

Chapter 10

Effects of Political Problems
on National Development

Development, as earlier described, is when a group of human species in a geographical location acquires the capacities to understand natural law that enables them to collectively organize to increase their capacity of production through technological innovations[1]. From classical to development economist, scholars have vigorously canvassed the theories, policies, and issues of development. Such early scholars as Walt Rostow, Gabriel Almond, Wilbert Moore and Cecil Blake have used the industrialized western countries as the prototypes for modernization. Such development economists as Arthur Lewis, Immanuel Wallerstein, Roy Harrod, David Ricardo, Walter Rodney, Ferdinando Cardoso and Enzo Falletto have propounded other theories to explore issues of development and their effects on developing nations and the world at large.

The modernization theory assumes that the development process is an accumulation of social changes that readies and culminates to the democratization of a nation. Essentially, the modernization theory conceptualizes development as a movement along a continuum of historical changes that all nations follow[2]. The modernists argue that this continuum is the path of societal evolution that has been followed by the developed nations, and should ultimately be traveled by the underdeveloped countries[3].

From the political perspectives of the modernization theory, the key to political development is an electorate that is both willing and able to participate in domestic politics[4]. Thus political participation plays a crucial role in economic development[5]. The thrust of the postulations of some modernization scholars is that genuine democracy is most likely to improve the level of development, improve income inequalities and improve standards of education[6].

In contemporary concepts, modernization could be described as a process in which underdeveloped countries catch up with the developed countries, not only in the context of economy but also in relations to politics, social life, and technology[7]. From the western perspective, therefore, the indices of modernization would include high gross national product and income per capita; and acceptance of "modern" values, social differentiation, and political integration.

Up until the late sixties, development was equated with economic growth; and Gross Domestic Product (GDP), Gross National Product (GNP), and income per capita were the main criteria for measuring development. Starting from the 1970s, however, other indicators of development have emerged through the works of development economists. Development is more comprehensive than economic growth; the latter is essentially a part of the former[8].

Development implies the transformation of poor and unindustrialized countries to developed and industrialized countries[9]. Such concepts as the provision of basic needs, creation of employment, and achievement of more equitable income distribution have become criteria for evaluating the level of development that exists in a nation[10]. Obviously, a strong democratic political culture can be highly supportive of efforts to address development problems; thereby establishing the basis for sustainable economic growth[11]. Democracy improves economic development; which in turn spreads authority and democratic aspirations among variety of people, thereby further fostering democracy[12].

Development is inherently beneficial to societies and should be promoted through the removal or degradation of the various obstacles to development. Some of the internal political factors obstacles that have adversely affected the development of Nigeria include the abuses of the political system, the neopatrimonial governance, effects of corruption, political conflicts, and political disruption of public policies.

Dysfunctional Political System

Certain aspects of democracy that include electoral competition and presence of credible opposition lead to improvements in political leadership. Seymour Martin Lipset had argued in *Political Man: The Social Bases on Politics* that the stability of the democratic system depends on the effectiveness and legitimacy of the political system that includes the executive, legislative, and judiciary arms of governance[13]. In Nigeria, there are massive, recurrent, and nationwide abuses of the political system. The most blatant is the manipulation of the electoral system. Elections are blatantly rigged in favor incumbents. There is massive abuse of state power, harassment of opposition candidates, and naked subordination of the judiciary. The arising dysfunctional political institutions and governance bears a substantial part of the blame for much of the disappointing economic performances and lack of developmental strategies in the country. These political distortions manifests in the prevalence of political and bureaucratic corruption.

As a positive example, experts have indicated that a large part of the gains in the economic development of Mauritius is attributable to the political system that has the politically established the basic institutional framework for organizing politics and governance that enhance inter-group relations and benefits[14].

Effects of Corruption

A major constraint to the development of Nigeria is the prevalence of political and bureaucratic corruption. Corruption in Nigeria is endemic, and the country has been consistently indexed by Transparency International as one of the mostly corrupt countries in the World. Corruption is highly detrimental to Nigeria as it leads to misallocation of resources, disrupts economic development and distorts public policies.

High levels of corruption mark political leadership in Nigeria. The political elites embezzle from national treasury for personal use, thereby undermining the accumulation of financial capital resources needed for economic development.

The problem of corruption in Nigeria also extends through all layers of bureaucracy, including customs, and police[15]. Corruption is not only detrimental to the society; but to business as well[16]. Essentially, corruption inhibits the desired outcomes of democracy and development[17].

In Nigeria, the weakness of the state institutions in

combating corruption, combined with the personalized patronages that hover over state institutions, only further go to encourage corruption. The pervading situation becomes that social and economic advancement become dependent on relationship to political power rather than competence and the effective use of economic resources. Adequate attention to political and bureaucratic corruption and its adverse effects on the development of Nigeria must, therefore, come to fore when considerations are made on the political and governance issues in the country.

Political Conflicts and Political Instability

For the state to develop, both internal and external stabilities are imperative. The stability or instability of the political process could promote or wreck the growth prospects of a country[18]. The countries that have invested in those policies and institutions that have increased their ability to manage and reduce social tensions have experienced lower levels of political instability[19].

Democracy as a system involving political conflicts between competing interests is nurtured and sustained only and only if the conflicts are resolved lawfully and peacefully[20]. The hallmark of a genuine democracy, therefore, is the ability to resolve the problems of leadership and succession through elections, without turmoil[21]. Unfortunately, political instability and ethnic conflicts have remained prominent parts of the political and social landscape of Nigeria; and ethnic fragmentation is responsible for a significant part of its political instability and public acceptance of corruption.

Absence of Genuine Electoral Competition

As the constructs of modern democracy must be

attentive to the system through which people compete for votes, a critical issue in Nigeria is the absence of genuine electoral competition. With the political leaders not been dependent on the electorate to win elections, the integrity of the electoral process in Nigeria is, next to nothing.

Obviously, the tendency of political leaders to stifle the opposition and the subsequent lack of viable opposition in Nigeria is largely a consequence of the authoritarian rules of the past decades. Without this credible threat of replacements through genuine electoral competitions, elected officials have fewer incentives to provide public goods. This state of affairs has had adverse effects on the development of the nation, because, the fundamental differences in the public-welfare disposition and development performance among democratic regimes are essentially outcrops of the whether or not electoral competition is restricted. Combined with such democratic deficits as non-accountability of elected officials, disregard for the rule of law, violations of human rights, and election malpractices, the integrity of the entire democratic process in Nigeria is, to say the least, highly questionable.

Poor and Unethical Political Leadership

The economic development of a nation is a complex phenomenon where success or failure depends on the determination and political will of its leadership. As with the absence of genuine democratic culture, lack of national vision, and weak political institutions; poor and unethical leadership, also undermines Nigeria's development[22].

As earlier indicated, the existing governing system with strong executive, central revenue control system, weak law and order institutions, and dysfunctional and corrupt bureaucracy makes it difficult to address Nigeria's development problems.

With the neopatrimonial nature of governance immensely contributing to the failures of the state as the agents of development, it becomes difficult to be optimistic. This is because states in which corruption and neopatrimonialism are prevalent suffer in relations to modernization as political opportunism rather than developmental objectives tend to drive policymaking. Worse still, the personalized distribution of state resources is leveraged over the welfare-enhancing public goods and services, thereby diverting the limited resources for development into private hands.

Political Disruption of Public Policies

Economic policy coherence, public-service effectiveness, and limited corruption are central to the development prospects of Nigeria. The public policymaking and administration in Nigeria is, however, politicized; leading to incoherent public policies and ineffective implementation of public policies. Combining with widespread public corruption, public policy in Nigeria generally leader-centered and has few mechanisms of accountability[23].

Obviously, coherent policy formulation, effective public administration, and limited corruption would enhance the developmental governance of Nigeria[24]. A pathway to development could be to compel political elites to adopt governance strategies that match political motivations to the requirements of economic development. Another development enhancing strategy would require the insulation of policymaking and implementation from arbitrary political interference[25].

Lack of Political and Public Accountability

The sustenance and consolidation of democracy requires that it be accountable to the people as well as respectful of the law[26]. Stable democracies require that genuine democratic practices be built upon the rule of law in which the constitution is supreme; where all citizens are equal before the law and the judiciary is independent from political influence[27].

Public and political accountability demands that elected or appointed officials, as well as the institutions charged with public mandate account for their actions, activities, or decisions to the public[28]. Generally, political accountability is best promoted through both state and non-state actors[29]. As political accountability increases, the political and legal costs to public officials who embark on corrupt practices increase[30].

This political and public accountability could be horizontal accountability measures as electoral competition, separation of powers, and legislative checks and balances; or vertical accountability as oversight by civil societies and the media[31].

Weak Judiciary and Property Rights Protection

The consideration for the effectiveness of the legal framework of a country includes the analysis of the independence of the judiciary, the impartiality of the courts, the protection of property rights and intellectual property, and the integrity of the legal system.

The protection of private property rights is of immense importance as the main basis for the economic development in the western world seems to be a well-developed property rights system. This is because, economic specialization, which is the main ingredient of modernization, requires well-defined property rights[32]. As Hernando De Soto (2001) indicated in *The mystery of capital: Why capitalism triumphs in the West and fails everywhere else,* the characteristics that the third world countries have in common is a very underdeveloped property rights system and legal apparatus[33].

Nigeria does not have strong and enforceable laws and regulations that offer adequate protection for property and contractual rights, and law enforcement is also often poor. The weaknesses of the judiciary in Nigeria have, therefore, continued to undermine the rule of law; remain sources of concern; and constitute deterrents to would-be foreign investors.

Mismanagement of Natural Resources

When a government finances its activities through taxation, it tends to interact and negotiate with the citizens; giving the citizens more opportunities to hold the government accountable[34]. When, however, the government of a country derives much of its funding from the export of natural resources, it confers the leaders with much power, facilitates neopatrimonialism, and enables the pursuit of self-agenda. The country is likely to experience more corruption, adversary competition for power, or political and civil conflicts. Economically, the country embarks on massive importation; domestic manufacturing is undermined; weakening the opportunities for human capital development, which further degenerates to massive unemployment. This tendency of such natural resources as oil to produce poor development and political outcomes is called the "Dutch curse" or 'resource curse'.

This "resource curse" is generally seen as been consistent with dysfunctional political systems[35]. This is because, whereas natural resources have provided the foundation for economic growth in the United States, Canada, Australia and Norway; it has only produced dependent economies, corruption, "clientelism," and authoritarian political systems in Nigeria, Venezuela, and Bolivia. The success of United States, Canada, Australia and Norway; and hence, the disparities in outcomes arise from the development of the resources and utilization of the revenues from the natural resources under the accountability compelled by genuine democratic institutions and practices. Essentially, when good political incentives and accountability are absent, natural resources production does not produce positive externalities[36].

Using Human Development Index to compare Nigeria with some African Countries

The United Nations Development Program (UNDP) states that the three basic aspects of human development are; leading a long and healthy life, being knowledgeable and enjoying a decent standard of living[37]. This thus, elevates educational attainment, health standards, and income per capita as the main indicators of development as measured by Human Development Index[38].

The human development index (HDI) is a summary index that measures a country's average achievements in three basic aspects of human development-health, knowledge, and a decent standard of living[39]. Health is measured by life expectancy at birth, knowledge by a combination of adult literacy and gross school enrollment ratio, and standard of living by GDP per capita in the US dollar-based purchasing power parity[40].

In the table 4 below, the data for Nigeria in 2000 was unavailable but was imputed through linear interpolation[41].

Table 4

Countries	Human Development Index (HDI)					
	2000	2005	2007	2010	2011	2012
Ghana	0.461	0.491	0.506	0.540	0.553	0.558
S. Africa	0.622	0.604	0.609	0.621	0.623	0.629
Mauritius	0.676	0.708	0.720	0.732	0.735	0.737
Botswana	0.587	0.604	0.619	0.633	0.634	0.634
Nigeria	0.390	0.434	0.448	0.462	0.467	0.471
Kenya	0.447	0.472	0.491	0.511	0.515	0.519
Benin	0.380	0.414	0.420	0.432	0.434	0.436
Zambia	0.376	0.399	0.411	0.438	0.443	0.448

Graph 5, representing the HDI of these countries gives a clearer picture of the comparison with Nigeria.

Graph 5

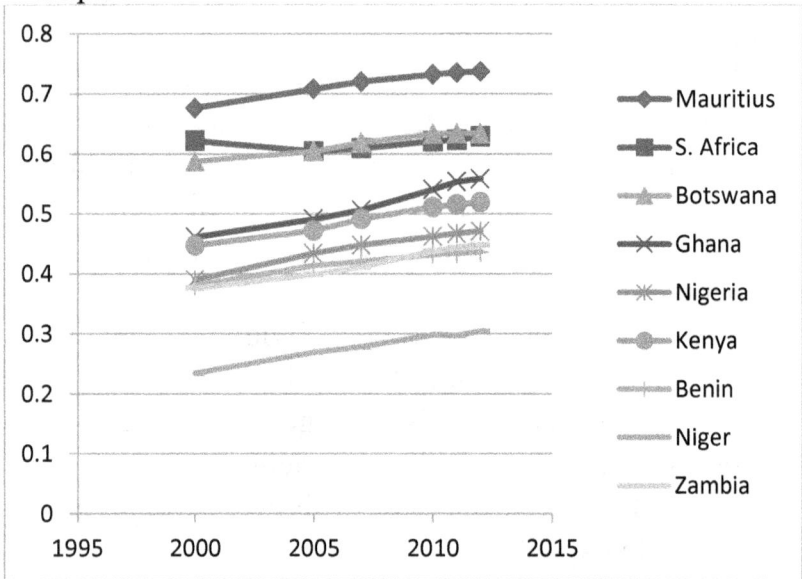

PART V

Elections, Political Leadership, and National Development.

Chapter 11

Elections and Political Leadership Performance

The democratic theory is hinged on the ability to hold organized elections through the power of votes, foster participation, encourage credible opposition, hold elected officials accountable, and protect the political and civil rights of citizens. Under democracy, the construct of leadership, elevates the reign of public safety and rule of law, protects the political and civil rights of the citizenry, creates economic opportunities, and strives to reduce and control corruption[1].

Achieving genuine democracy and effective leadership requires that competition among political parties should create and foster more responsive governance by encouraging elected leaders to commit to service and accountability. Being an electoral democracy should also mean that the electoral process is highly protected as to ensure free and fair elections. Hence, the fair and open elections in which the performances of elected officials are subjected to the ultimate evaluation are most important to the success or failure of a democracy[2].

Under the democratic system, voters are expected to reward good leadership and punish poor performances. Although the voters have limited means for checking the behavior of elected leaders, elections generally allow them to re-elect or throw out the incumbent representatives and officials. This ability to re-elect or throw out elected official does not depend exclusively on the real, anticipated or perceived performance of the incumbent but also on the anticipated performance of the opposition[3]

Arising from the concerns of the elected official on this possibility of losing voters' support to the opposition, electoral competition makes the political leadership to be more responsive and more accountable[4]. Therefore, accountability cannot exist without the requisite competition[5]. Moreover, the political competition that is accompanied by repeated elections generates a credible threat of replacement, creates a balance between the politician, expected to provide good leadership performance and the citizens who demand the same.

Electoral competition, therefore, offers the advantage of rooting public policies in political accountability[7]. Moreover, by encouraging public accountability, electoral competition imposes checks on the leadership[8]. In ideal democratic settings, when incumbent governments sense that the opposition is strong and credible enough to take power, they act in ways that would enhance public satisfaction with their activities[9].

Electoral competition is, therefore, a defining mechanism for democracy as it creates and guarantees accountability, imposes constraints on executive, and encourages leadership responsiveness to the governed; thereby improving the performance of presidential leadership . Electoral competition fosters responsiveness and accountability, improves quality of governance, enhances political stability, induces human rights protection, and encourages credible opposition.

The conduct of genuine electoral competition brings improvement in leadership by incentivizing leaders to deliver on public goods and services. Electoral competition, therefore, relates to improvements in such governance quality dimension as economic policy cohesion, public service effectiveness, and limited corruption. Thus, when performance is measured in terms of spending on welfare of the citizenry, genuine electoral competition improves governance[10]. There are, hence, positive effects of electoral competition on indicators of political leadership performance[11]. Obviously, some governance qualities, political, and policy incentives can only be canvassed through improvements in the quality of governance that can be improved through improvement in the level of electoral competition.

As genuine democracy and good governance go together, then electoral competition and political leadership performance will share positive relationships. These ideals of electoral competition being true, then prospects for countries where groups of citizens with different social interests can organize parties and promote candidates for election to public office under genuine conducts of elections is highly desirable.

In a country like Nigeria, where real competition among political parties is not well-enough established as to be effective, there is, however, little incentive for leaders or would-be leaders to devote themselves to the high ideals of service and accountability. Moreover, rather than responding to the electorate by improving public services, Nigerian presidents usually resort to self-centered patronage and electoral manipulations.

Hence, electoral competitions in Nigeria have not

always attained the levels desirable for elevating the leaders toward such higher ideals as service and accountability. This absence of genuine electoral competition in the political system of Nigeria has had adverse effects on the political leadership performances in the nation.

Genuine electoral competition creates the good governance; and does not only contribute to transparency and accountability in government operations, but also create sustainable economic environment for both the citizens and foreign investors; thereby enhancing national development.

There is an urgent need to increase the quality of leadership in Nigeria. To achieve this, the democratic process must be genuinely democratic; reducing social and ethnic tensions by, respecting the sovereignty, and electoral desires of the people. Obviously, electoral turn-overs and declining legislative dominance by one party do have positive effects on electoral competition[12].

Comparing the genuineness of the elections using the of Polity IV score and the political leadership performance using the World Governance Index (WGI) between Nigeria and some African countries gives a clearer picture of this relationship as shown in graphs 6, 7, and 8 below.

Stable and Consolidated Democracies

As the graphs 6a, 6b, and 6c show, such countries as Mauritius, South Africa, and Botswana that have continually practiced the higher ideals of genuine electoral competition have either continuously experienced improvements or have maintained high leadership performances.

(a) Mauritius

Graph 6a

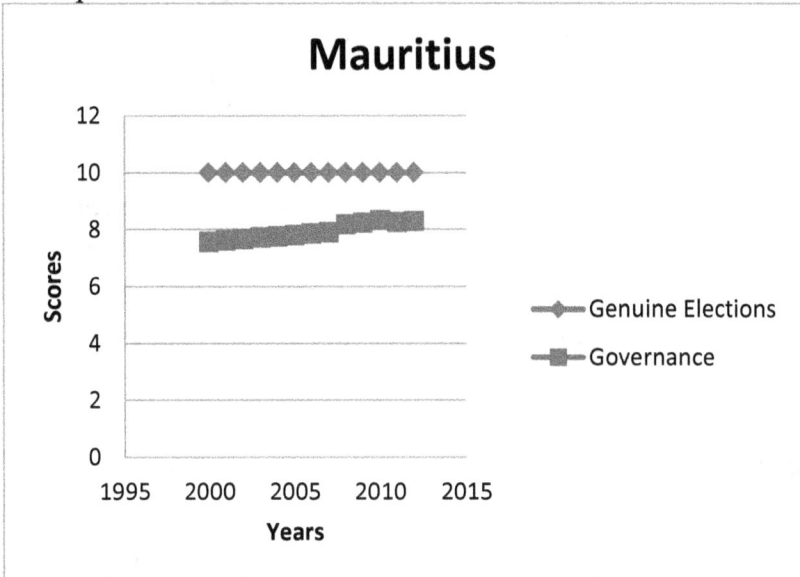

Mauritius

Since independence in 1968, Mauritius has always selected its prime minister through multi-party elections. Mauritius has a parliamentary system of governance, in which the leader of the majority party (or majority coalition) becomes selected by the elected members of the national assembly as the prime minister.

At the time of independence, the prospects of political stability seemed bleak for Mauritius as ethnic pluralism and economic stagnation led to communal and ethnic violence. Over the years, however, Mauritius has become one of the most stable and democratic nations in Africa; with very impressive economic and human development growth. Also, Mauritius has continuously maintained the best leadership performance in Africa as judged both by the World Governance Indicators and Mo Ibrahim Leadership Index for Africa.

(b) **South Africa**

Graph 6b

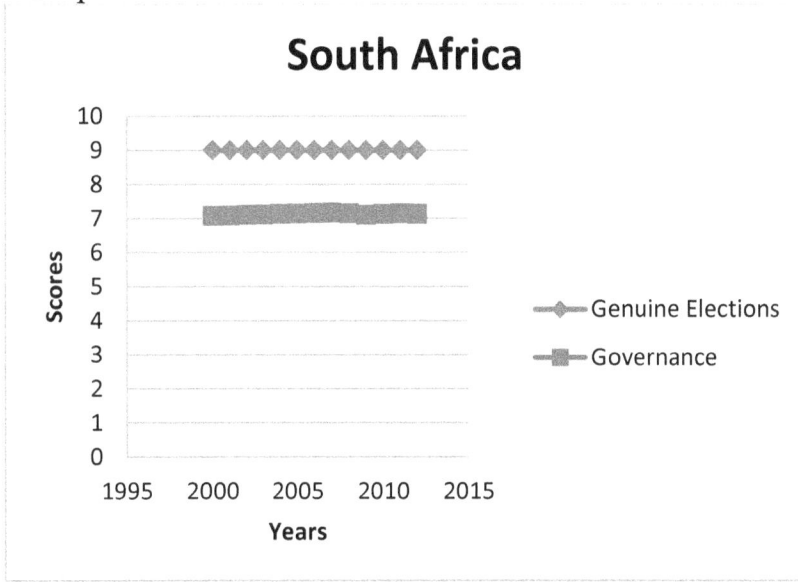

The election in 1994, of Nelson Mandela as the president of South Africa brough an end to the 'racial democracy' of the apatheid system. The political system of government in South Africa tends to combine the presidential and parliamentary systems. For instance, whereas the president is chosen by the national assembly as in the parliamentary system, he/she is not directly accountable to the legislature.

Although the African National Congress (ANC) has dominated the political landscape, elections have always been through competitive multiparty system. Despite the fact that the problems of inequality and corruption have begun to creep into the political system, South Africa remains a state in which civil and political rights of the citizens are respected.

(c) Botswana

Graph 6c

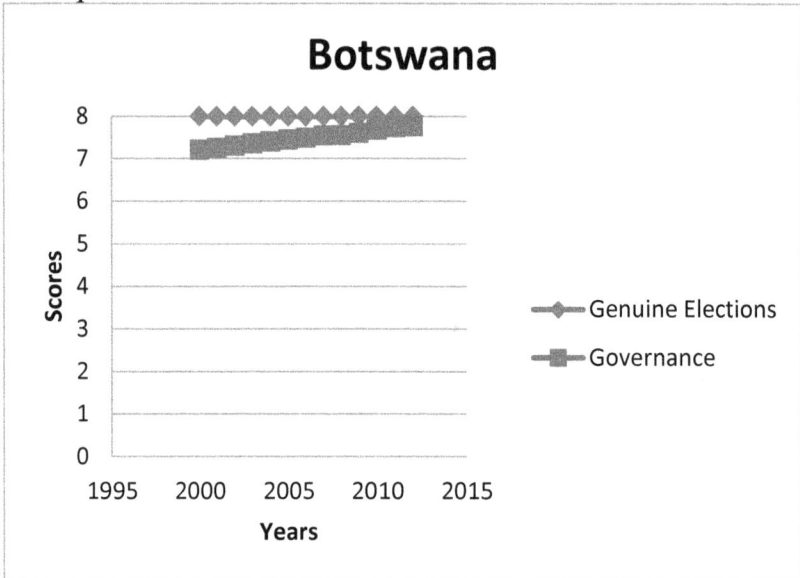

Since gaining independence from Britain in 1966, Botswana has elected her chief executive officer through multiparty elections with the majority party in the national assembly selecting the president for 5-year terms. As in South Africa, the political system in Botswana places some constraints on the president, who, although not accountable to the national assembly, is nonetheless, chosen by the national assembly. Although the Botswana Democratic Party (BDP) dominates the political landscape, the country is still reputed as a beacon of political stability in Africa.

(ii) **Consolidating democracies**

Such other countries as Ghana and Zambia that were previously under dictatorships; but thereafter, experienced dramatic improvements in levels of electoral competition; have experienced corresponding improvement in political leadership performances.

(a) Ghana

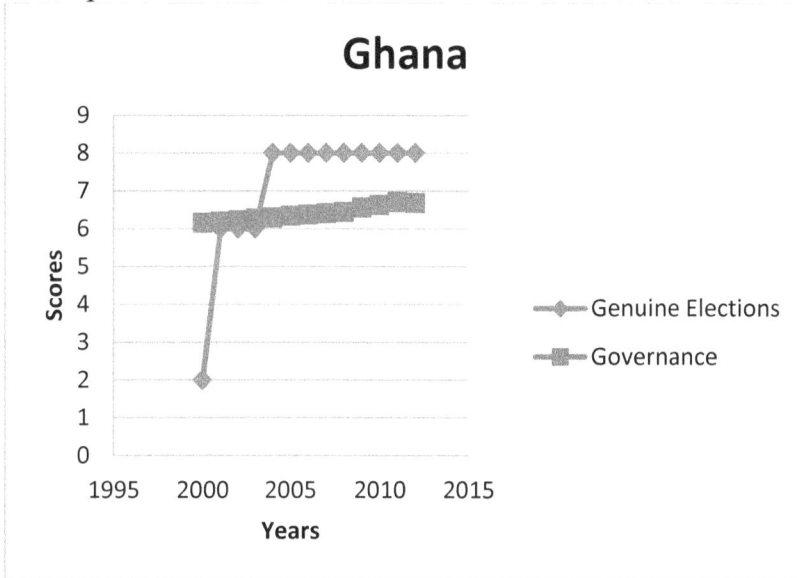

Ghana

Legend:
- Genuine Elections
- Governance

The december 2000 elections in Ghana marked a watershed in the country's political life as the presidential candidate of the incumbent National Democratic Congress (NDC), John Atta Mills lost to the candidate of the opposition New Patriotic Party (NPP), John Kufour. The NDC was the incumbent party and was led by term-limited and out-going president, Jerry Rawlings. This election marked an important transition from an electoral authoritarianism to more open and genuine electoral competitions. In furtherance of the new culture of open and genuine electoral competition, the candidate of the now ruling NPP, Nana Akuffo-Addo, in 2008, lost to the now oppostion NDC candidate, John Mills. This second electoral turn-over of an incumbent party losing a presidential election to the opposition party brought Ghana into the league of consolidated democracies.

Graph 7b

Zambia

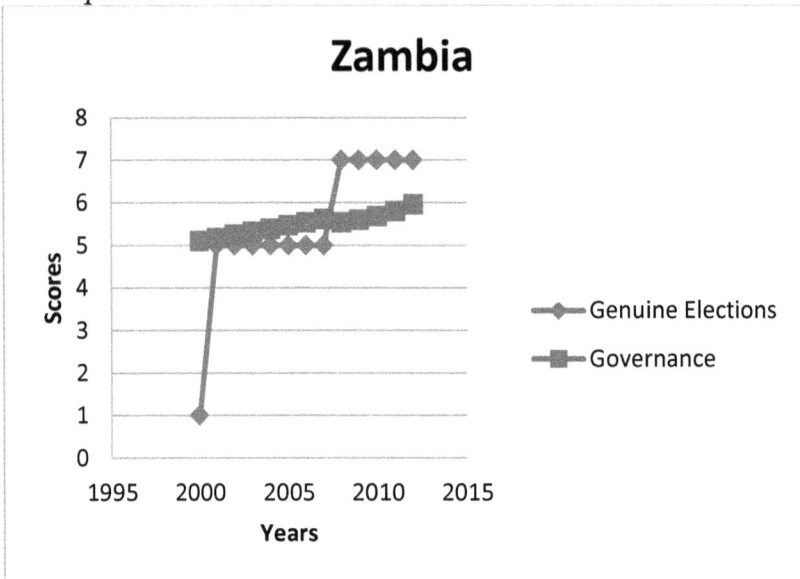

The United National Independence Party (UNIP) of Kenneth Kaunda ruled from independence in 1963. The lost of the presidency by Dr Kennth Kaunda to the opposition candidate of the Movement for Multiparty Democracy (MMD), Frederick Chiluba in October, 1991 started the match of Zambia to multiparty and competitive electoral democracy. The hope of consolidating this democracy, however, withered as President Chiluba sought to concentrate power through the use of emergency decrees, control of media, and self-serving constitutional amendments that banned former president Kenneth Kaunda from seeking elections to the presidency. Chiluba even made protracted efforts to re-wrtie the constitution and allow himself a third term of presidency.

Chiluba's term-elongation efforts were furtile; and in a 27 december, 2001 election, a Chiluba protegee, Levy

Mwanawasa, of the ruling MMD was elected as the president. International observers and monitors indicated that although the elections were not overtly fraudulent, the incumbent government distorted the playing field in favour of the candidate of the ruling party by giving them control over state-run media. The MMD did not, however, have overwhelming legislative majority; and the one-party dominance that charectarized the regimes of Kenneth Kaunda and Federick Chiluba effectively came to an end.

President Mwanawasa was re-elected on 28 september 2006 but died on August 19 2008, after suffering a stroke as he attended the African Union summit meeting in Egypt. In an election held on 30 october 2008 to complete Mwanawasa's term, the candidate of the incumbent MMD, Rupiah Banda won by a narrow margin.

In the next presidential election of 20 september 2011, however, the opposition candidate of the Patriotic Front (PF), Michael Sata won the presidency. This electoral turn-over from the incumbent MMD to the opposition PF further consolidated Zambia's democracy.

ii) **Electoral Authoritarianism**

As graph 8 depicts, Nigeria has been stagnant at the lower levels of electoral competition; and has subsequently remained at the lower levels of political leadership performance.

Graph 8

Nigeria

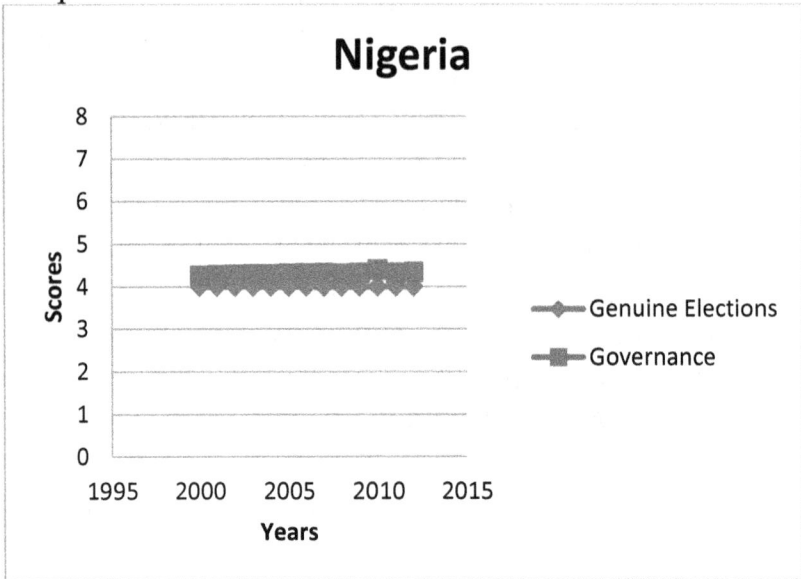

Prior to 2000, the blatantly ethnic-based military rulers in Nigeria played a destabilizing role on democracy. The overt political ambitions of senior military officers, coupled with ethnic-based factional tensions, as well as endemic corruption thwarted efforts at establishing genuine democratic institutions.

After the election of Olusegun Obasanjo of the People's Democratic Party (PDP) in February, 1999, subsequent elections have been marred by one-party domination, electoral fraud, and political tensions. President Obasanjo's regimes were seriously marred by general insecurity, political in-fighting, intimidation of the opposition, and political assassinations. President Obasanjo even made efforts to amend the constitution to allow him a third term; but the efforts were futile.

The election, on the 21st April 2007, that marked the first civilian-to- civilian, but same-party transition, in which Umaru Musa Yar' Adua of the ruling PDP was elected was seriously marred by electoral improprieties.

Following the death of President Yar' Adua on the 6th may, 2010, however, the vice president, Dr Goodluck Ebele Jonathan was sworn in as the president. Against the background of a purported but non-constitutionalized zoning system, a quest by President Jonathan to seek his own first term under the same ruling PDP, made the North-South dichotomy a significant political issue again.

The concentration of political power in the presidency makes the competition for control of the federal government in Nigeria a zero-sum win-lose situation, rather than the integrative quality of win-win for all citizens. Nigeria's democracy, therefore, continues to be plagued by ethnic frictions; economic wants and scarcity, and religious conflicts and polarization; and most recently by religious fundamentalism.

For these, electoral competition in Nigeria remains at very low levels; and subsequently, the political leadership performance remains one of the poorest in the democratic countries of Sub-Saharan Africa. To begin the journey toward substantially improving political leadership performance and subsequently improving human development levels, Nigeria would need to improve its level of electoral competition.

Chapter 12

Political Leadership Performance and National Development

Development, which has been described as is the collective organization of a group of human species who have acquired the capacities to understand natural law; enabling them to organize for the purpose of increasing capacity of production through technological innovations, also has political underpinnings[1]. The economic development of a nation is a complex phenomenon in which outcomes are largely dependent on the political performance of leadership. Effective leadership is, therefore, one of the most critical prerequisites for national economic development; and the role of leaders and leadership in economic development cannot be overlooked. Existentially, the poor economic record of a nation may be attributable to leadership problems.

Although both the modernization and dependency theories suggest that developing countries have potential capacities for economic development through industrialization, both theories were salient on questions of leadership[2]. As leadership constitutes the acts and processes designed to influence people to direct their efforts toward the achievement of some particular goal or performance, it also has some relationship with the prospects for human development. This is because, effective leaders are able to shape public policy in a way that aligns their own personal ambitions and talents with the economic and social needs and desires of the people they serve.

In essence, a leadership that creates institutions that align political incentives with developmental objectives is more likely to develop more constructive public policies. Good political leadership in a developing nation would entail protection of human rights, enthronement of rule of law, enhancing public safety, creating sustainable economic opportunities for the citizens, investment in human development, and definite and concise efforts to control corruption.

Obviously, political development is central to the sustenance of social and economic development. When the political process is ineffective, social and economic development are retarded[3]. Faltering democratic leadership could lead to violent civil conflicts, military usurpation of power, arbitrary governance that does not uphold basic human rights and rule of law, or an unresponsive government that does not deliver public goods nor address the needs of the society[4].

Moreover, social and economic development depends on the existence of a political leadership environment that brings political incentives and the requirements for economic development into consonance. These political incentives can be canvassed only through improvements in the level of electoral competition.

As most development experts agree, the essence of the existence of a political environment that aligns political incentives with the requirements for economic development; the political outputs that have strong and direct impact on development include such factors as market-augmenting economic policies, political stability, efficient public service system, limited corruption, and rule of law. The political leaderships of Nigeria have, unfortunately, been marked by high levels of corruption. The political elites embezzle from national treasury for personal use; thereby undermining the accumulation of financial capital resources needed for economic development.

Obviously, the lagging development of the country has been attributed to leadership problems. For Nigeria to hasten its development, therefore, the prevailing political practices have to improve. For Nigeria, the qualities that should define presidential leadership performance would be; the level of public safety and rule of law; political and human rights; opportunities for sustainable economic development; and the control of corruption.

Using the world governance index and Human Development Index (HDI) to compare the political leadership performance and the level of national development in Nigeria with those of some other African countries gives a clearer picture of the situation. The countries have been categorized in the development groupings done by the United Nations Development Program (UNDP).

(i) High Development Nations

As the graph 9 shows, Mauritius, which has maintained high levels of political leadership performance, arising from their continual practice of the higher ideals of electoral competition has subsequently maintained improvements in national development.

(a) Mauritius

Graph 9

Mauritius

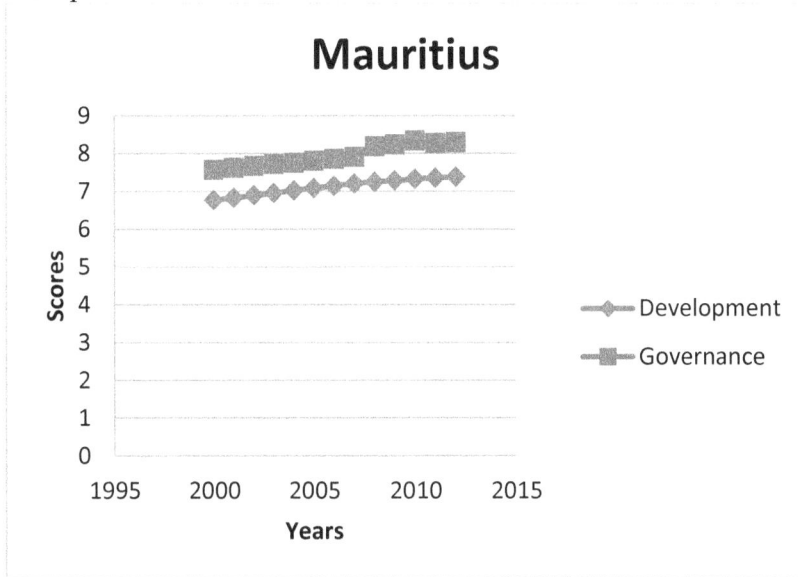

Mauritius has maintained a HDI above 0.65, putting the country in the league of high development nations. Political and economic scholars believe that the economic and political success of Mauritius has been the ability of the diverse ethnic groups in striking balances on their communal interests by forging alliances that mitigate ethnic and religious divides through parliamentsary compromise and coalition building as well as the vibrant civil societies that cut across ethnicity and religion.

(ii) Medium Development nations

As the graph 10a, b, and c show South Africa, Botswana, and Ghana, which, have experienced sustained net improvements in political leadership performance, arising from their strivings to higher ideals of electoral competition have subsequently experienced and maintained net improvements in national development.

(a)

Graph 10a

South Africa

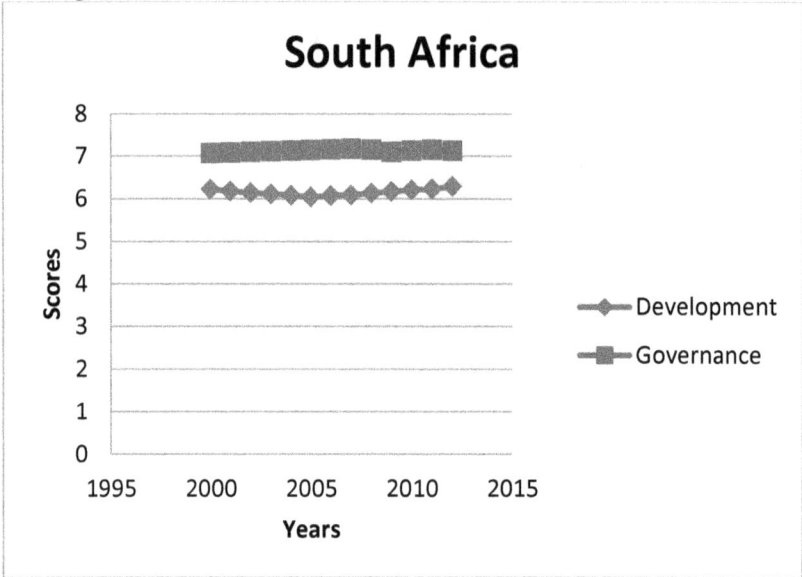

South Africa has maintained a HDI above 0.6, putting it in the category of medium development countries.

(c) **Botswana**:

Graph 10c

Botswana

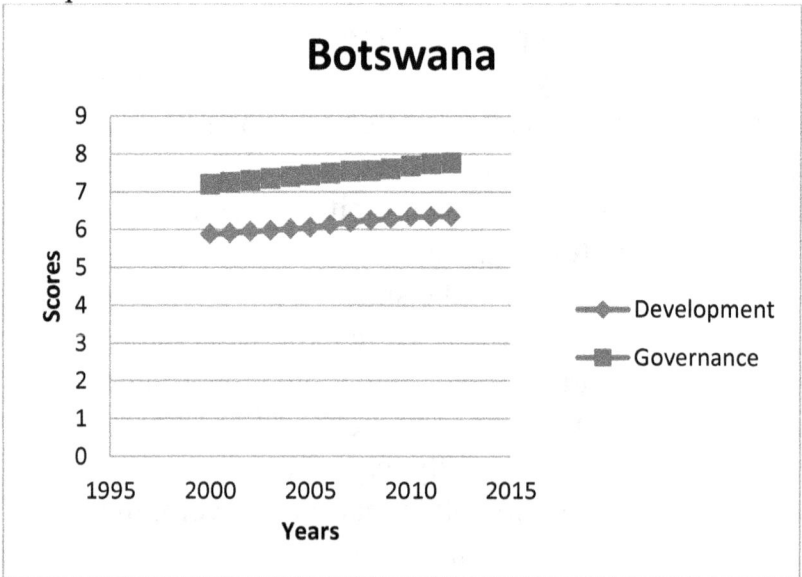

With the HDI above 0.6, Botswana is also a medium development nation.

(c) **Ghana**

As the graphical representation 10c shows, Ghana experienced improvements in political leadership and subsequently, experienced great improvement in human development. This is because Ghana had tremendously improved in the levels of electoral competition; and has subsequently experienced corresponding improvement in political leadership performances and national development.

Graph 10c

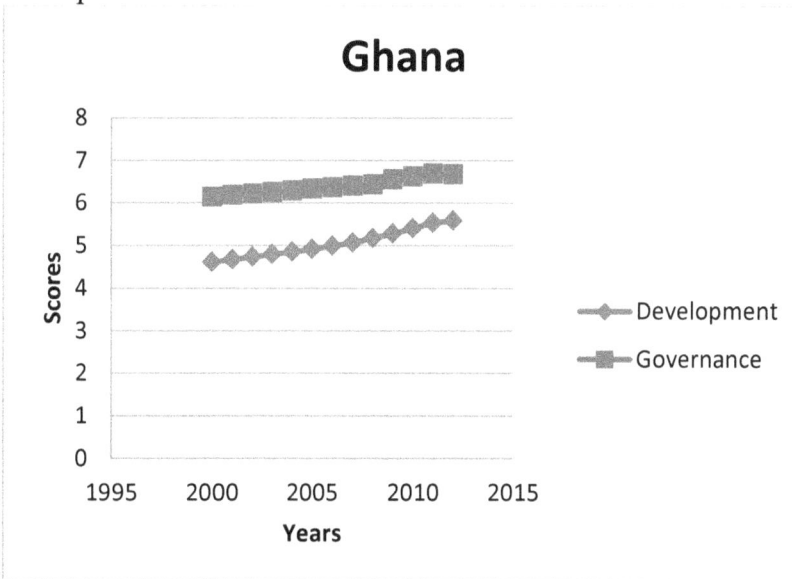

When Ghana improved to a polity score of 8 in 2004, its leadership performance began to improve, and subsequently its HDI rose from 0.5 in 2005 to 0.6 in 2011; elevating the country from the category of low development to medium development country.

(iii) **Zambia: Low but Improving Development**

As the graphical representation 11 shows that Zambia, which has experienced improvements in political leadership, has also experienced great improvement in human development. Zambia has tremendously improved in the levels of electoral competition; and has subsequently experienced corresponding improvement in political leadership performances and national development.

Graph 11

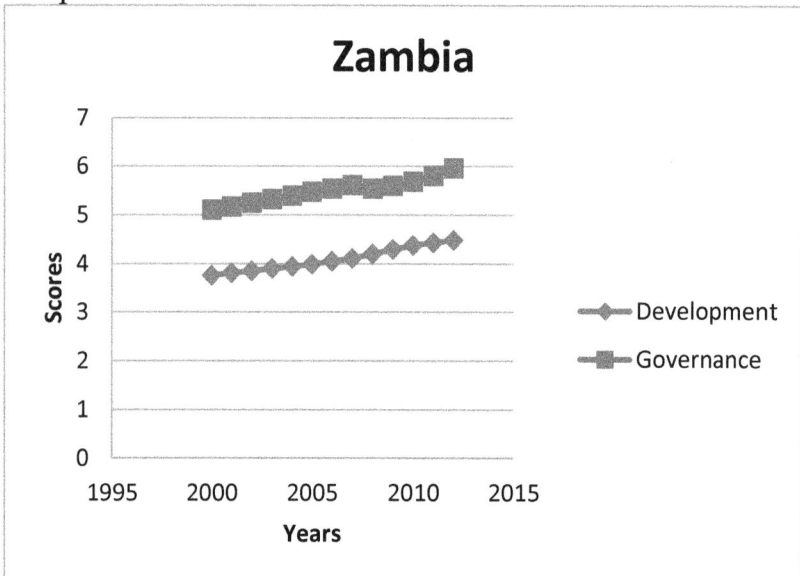

Although, Zambia remains in the category of low development, the country's HDI has risen sharply as the electoral competition and the political leadership performance improved.

(iii) **Nigeria : Low and Stagnant Development**

Nigeria, stagnating at the lower levels of electoral competition, and subsequently low levels of political leadership performance has remained indexed as a low development nation.

The HDI of Nigeria has remained below the 0.5, and has subsequently remained categorized as a low development nation as depicted in graph 12.

Graph 12

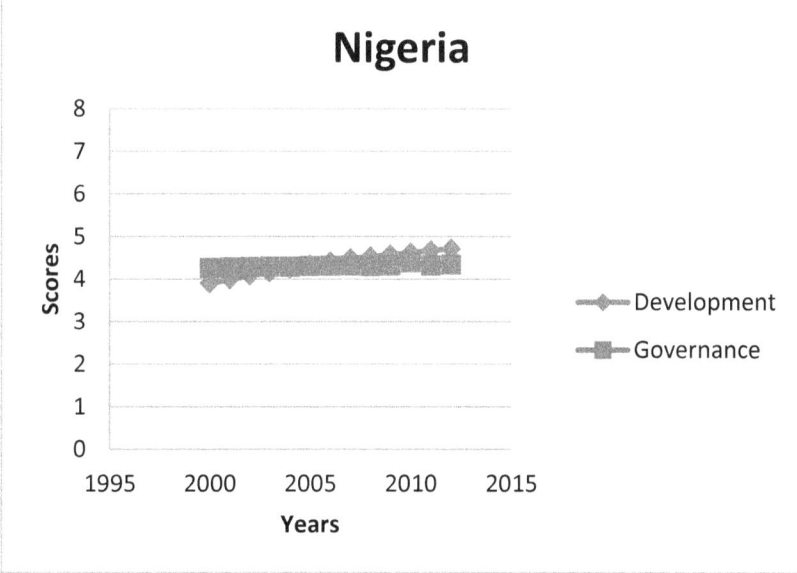

Nigeria

Chapter 13

Elections, Leadership, and National Development

There exists some links between electoral competitions, quality of leadership and national development of a democratic state. Electoral competition affects human development by pressuring elected officials to deliver public goods and services. An open and accountable electoral system is more likely to provide greater opportunity to foster effective political leadership and economic development. There are, therefore, positive relationships to genuine democratic elections in developing countries to such human development indicators as education and public services[1]. Genuine elections in developing democracies pressurize elected officials to promote human capital development through investments in healthcare and education; thus contributing to economic growth[2].

Elections conducted under the auspices of efficient and functioning political institutions, create good governance; which, contribute to transparency and accountability in government operations that further go to create positive images to foreign investors[3]. Genuine electoral competition is the aspect of democratic dispensation that is responsible for the positive spillovers of democracy on governance quality and improvement in human development. The elections involved in democratic governance, if genuine, positively influence the quality of leadership, which in turn, engineers improvements in national development.

Seymour Martin Lipset (1959) in *Some Social Requisites of Democracy: Economic Development and Political Legitimacy,* suggested a positive linear relationship between the levels of development and democratic development[4]. Furthermore, economic development involving industrialization, high educational standards and steady increase in the overall wealth of the society is a basic condition sustaining democracy[5]. The stability of the democratic system is dependent, not only on the efficiency of modernization, but also upon the effectiveness and legitimacy of the political system[6]. Moreover, when the performance is measured in terms of public services, democratic governance system in which electoral competition is genuine should clearly outperform authoritarian regimes because they reduce opportunities for rent-seeking behavior[7].

The predominant findings from quantitative comparative researches show positive correlation between socio-economic development and genuine electoral democratic practices[8]. The reasons for the positive impact of democracy and development is that this positive cycle of economic development, engineered by electoral competition, spreads authority and democratic aspirations among variety or people; thereby fostering the democracy that in turn furthers economic development[9]. Economic development that involves industrialization, urbanization, high educational standards, and steady improvement human living standards do not only sustain democracy, but are also the mark of the efficiency of the total system of the nation[10]. Although socioeconomic development is a necessary condition for the sustenance of a democratic system, the stability of the democratic system depends on legitimacy of the political system as well as the recognition, acceptance, and practice of democratic principles. The positive developmental outcomes of democracy in the Western countries are largely due to the high level of democratic competition in those countries; thus making democracy hold up as the pathway to modern development in such countries. Democracy in Nigeria has, on the contrary, yielded little or no positive effects on development of the country because the political practice is essentially electoral authoritarianism that restricts electoral competition. To join the western nations in reaping the positive benefits of democracy entails that electoral competitions in Nigeria must improve to credible levels. These dividends of democracy are only feasible in the democratic countries where elections are free, fair, and genuine.

Graphs 13, 14, 15, and 16 show the relationships between the level of electoral practices (genuine elections) as operationalized by the annual Polity Score (PS); the level of political leadership performance (Governance) as operationalized by Ibrahim Index of African Governance; and the level of national development (Development) as operationalized by Human development Index for Nigeria and some countries in Sub-Saharan Africa over the period 2000-2012.

The Ibrahim Index of African Governance was used here because it uses the assessments that are well-suited for the African nations as well as possessing the criteria used to assess leadership performance in Nigeria in chapter 15.

1. The Exemplary Nations

These are countries that have had polity scores of 8 or above for a long time period. They include Mauritius, South Africa, and Botswana. These countries have experienced the interwoven relationships among their high levels of electoral competition, the performance of political leaders, and improvements in the level of human development. At such moderately high levels of electoral competition, the political institutions are stable enough to withstand any occasional bad leadership. These countries also have high leadership performance indexes, and are in the high/medium development classification of the United Nations Development Programme (UNDP).

(a) Mauritius

Graph 13a

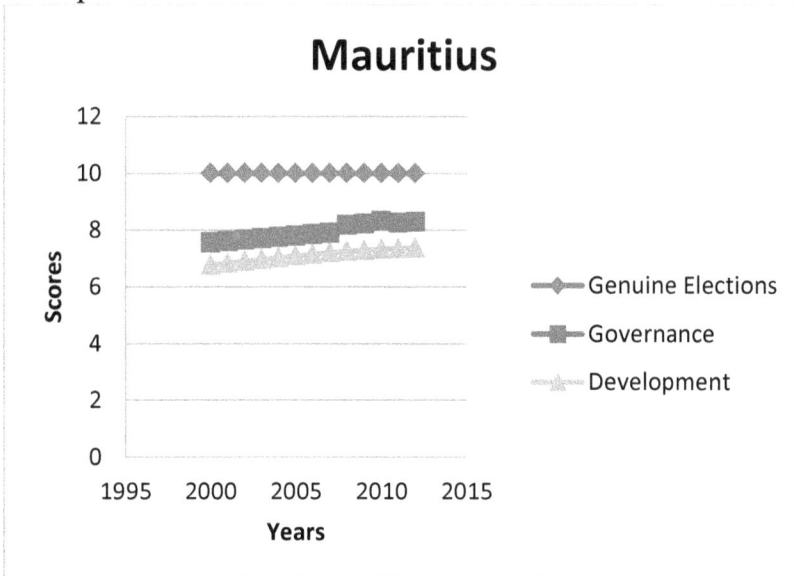

Mauritius

Mauritius has a polity score of 10 (out of 10), a leadership performance index of 8 (out of 10), and HDI of 0.74 (out of 1.0); and is therefore in the zone of high development countries.

As some studies have found, a large part of the gains in the economic development of Mauritius is attributable to the political system that has established institutional framework for organizing politics and governance that enhance inter-group relations and benefits[11].

(b)South Africa

Graph 13b

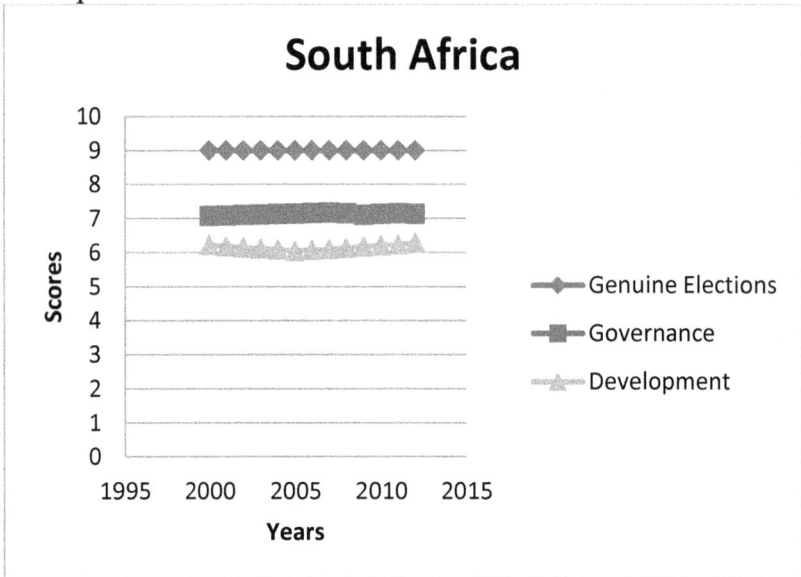

South Africa has a polity score of 9 (out of 10), a leadership performance index of 7 (out of 10), and HDI of 0.63(out of 1.0); and is therefore in the category of medium development countries.

(c)Botswana

Graph 13c

Botswana

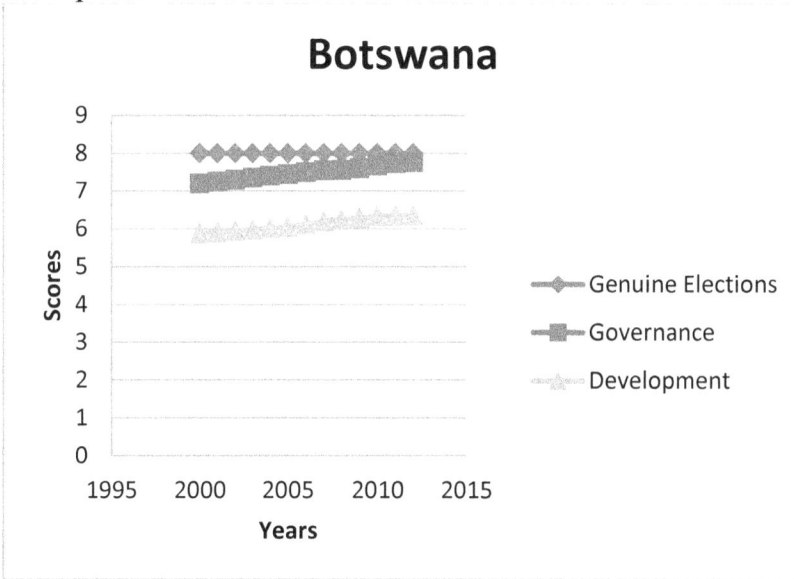

Botswana has a polity score of 8 (out of 10), a leadership performance index of 8 (out of 10), and HDI of 0.64 (out of 1.0); and is therefore in the category of medium development countries.

2. The Improving Nations

These countries have experienced dramatic improvement in their electoral competition as some incumbents and ruling parties have lost elections to the opposition. The improvements in their electoral competition have led to improvements in the levels of political leadership. These improvements have resulted to improvements in national developmement indexes; namely healthcare, educational attainment and standards of living; thereby transforming these countries in better societies.

(a) Ghana

Graph 14a

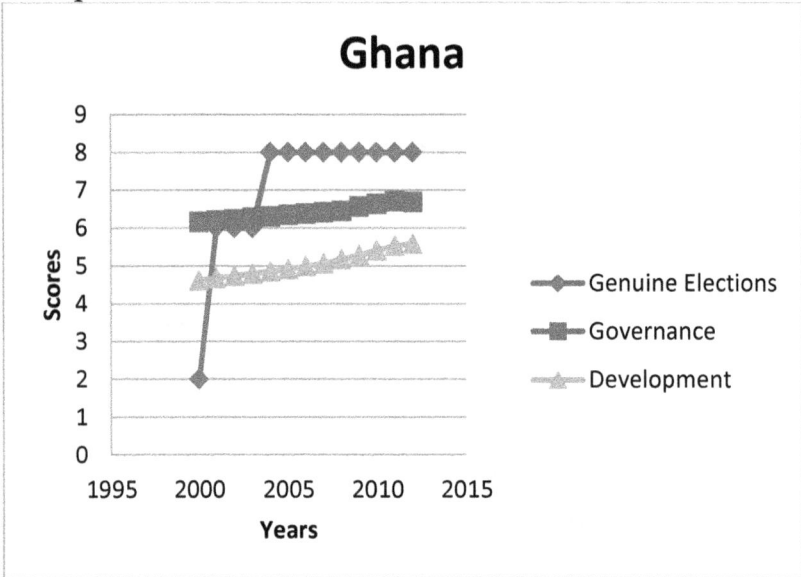

Ghana

Ghana leaped from a polity score of 2 in 2000 to a score of 8 in 2004. In that time period, the country's HDI rose substantially from 0.46 to 0.50. Ghana currently has a polity score of 8 (out of 10), a leadership performance index of 7 (out of 10), and HDI of 0.56 (out of 1.0); and is therefore in the category of medium development countries. Ghana experienced an improvement of about 22% of HDI from 2000 to 2012.

(b) Republic of Benin

Graph 14b

Benin

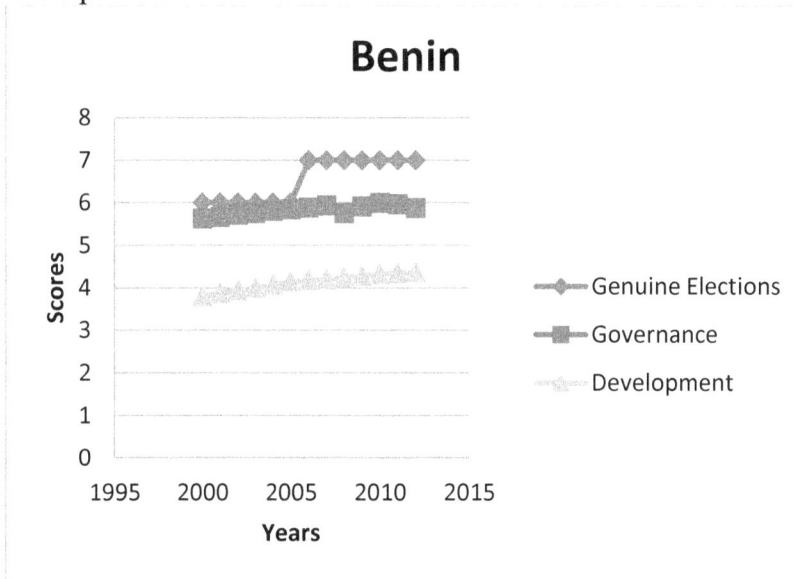

Benin republic experienced slight improvement in the level of electoral competition from "score 6" in 2000 to "score 7' in 2012. This led to corresponding improvements in performance of political leadership in the country; and a subsequent improvement of HDI from 0.38 in 2000 to 0.44 in 2012.

Benin has a polity score of 7 (out of 10), a leadership performance index of 5.9 (out of 10), and HDI of 0.44 (out of 1.0); an improvement of about 16% of HDI from 2000 to 2012.

(c) Zambia

Graph 14c

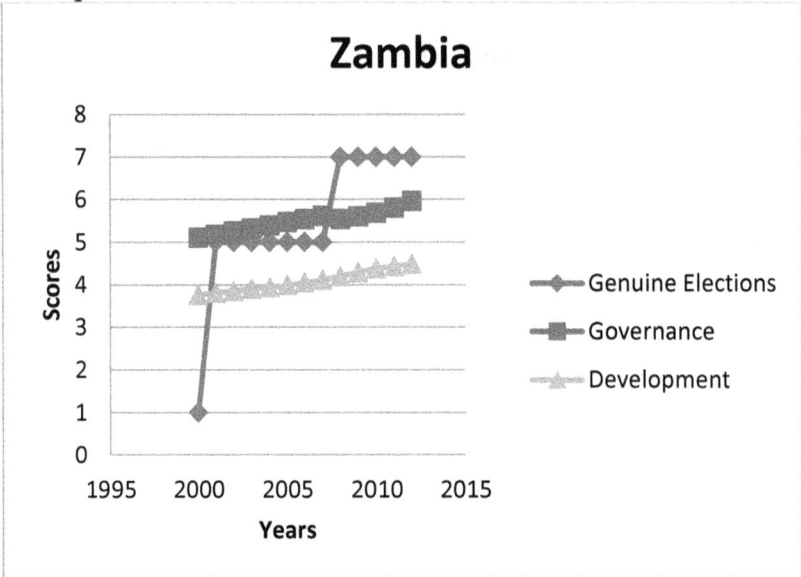

From the low point of 1 in the plotity score in 2000, Zambia experienced continous substatial improvements, cresting at 7 score in 2008. Subsequently, Zambia has experience improvement in the quality of political leadership with its resultant improvement in national development index from 0.38 in 2000 to 0.45 in 2012.

Zambia has a polity score of 7 (out of 10), a leadership performance index of 6.0 (out of 10), and HDI of 0.45 (out of 1.0). Although the country is still in the category of low development countries, it has experienced substantive improvement of about 18% of HDI from 2000 to 2012.

3. Kenya: Checkered Performance

Graph 15

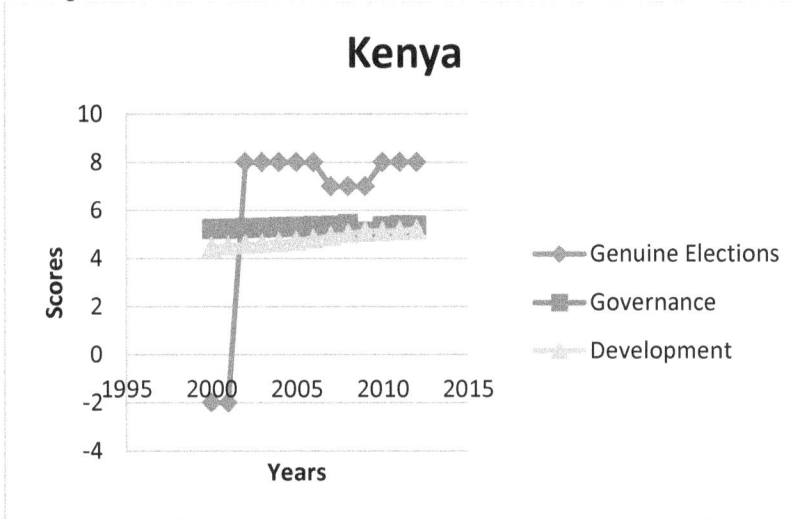

Kenya has had a checkered performance with its electoral processes. Kenya, however, leaped from a polity score of -2 in 2000 to a score of 8 in 2002, dropping a notch to score 7 in 2007, and rising agawarg to score 8 in 2010. Nonetheless, the leadership performance has improved enough as to improve her HDI substantially from 0.45 in 2000 to 0.52 in 2012.

Kenya currently has a polity score of 8 (out of 10), a leadership performance index of 5.4 (out of 10), and HDI of 0.52 (out of 1.0); and is therefore in the upper zone of the category of low development countries. Kenya experienced an improvement of about 16% of HDI from 2000 to 2012.

4. Nigeria: Stagnated Performance

Nigeria, as a restricted democracy or electoral authoritarianism has not made any substantial improvement in its electoral competition. Subsequently its political leadership performance has remained stalled at low levels; and there has not been any substantial improvement in the national development of the country. From the graph 15 below, it can be seen that the quality of elections, the performance of political leadership, and the human development in Nigeria has remained the lower levels.

Graph 16

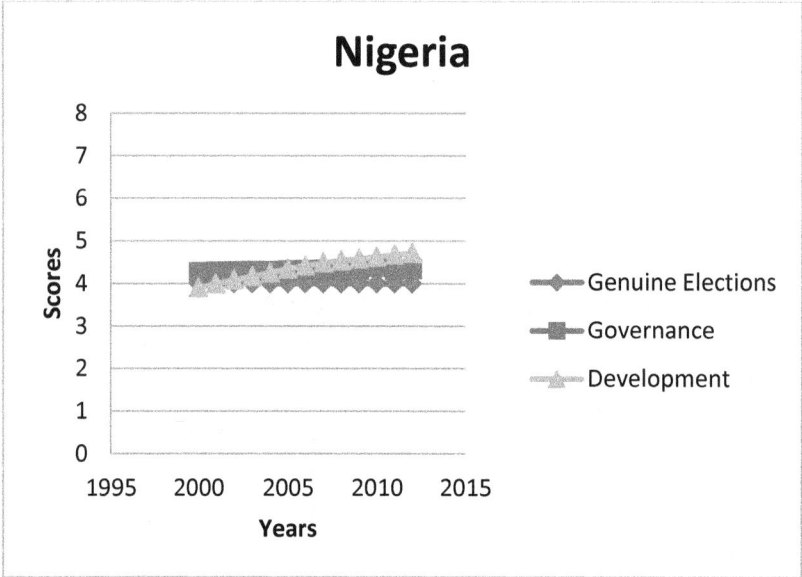

Nigeria has remained at the low mark of polity 4 score from 2000 to 2012 without any improvement. Consequently the leadership performance index for the same period has remained at 4.4 (out of 10) and the HDI negligibly from 0.44 to 0.47 between 2005 and 2012. Nigeria has, therefore, not experienced any substantial improvements in electoral competition, political leadership performance, and national development for the period of democratic rule. This also means that between 2005, when the positive effects of democracy should have been manifest, and 2012, the life expectancy (healthcare), literacy rate (educational attainment) and standards of living of Nigerians have remained stagnant.

Nigeria has a polity score of 4 (out of 10), a leadership performance index of 4.3 (out of 10), and HDI of 0.47 (out of 1.0); and in the category of low development countries. Expectedly, Nigeria experienced an abysymally low growth of about 0.6% of HDI from 2000 to 2012.

A complete examination of the Polity IV Cross-national database shows that the consolidated democracies that have polity scores of 8 or above have HDIs above 0.6 level; and are, at the least, in the category of medium development nations. This is because, when democracy is sustained over time, it influences development through the physical, human, social, and political capitalization[12]. As the quality of electoral practices improve, so does the political leadership performance; and subsequently so does the human development index of a nation.

Essentially, the quality of electoral competition has impact on the leadership of democratic nations. This improvement in presidential leadership performance, in turn, leads to improvement in the HDI of the country as reflected by literacy rate, life expectancy, and the standard of living. For Nigeria to begin to experience the values and benefits of democracy there must be improvements in electoral competitions in the country. Obviously, a reasonable line of action for Nigeria would be to embark on reforms that would improve the conducts of elections and subsequently the "polity score" of the country to 8, at the least. Some reform agenda are explained in chapter 21.

PART VI

Practices and Assessments

Chapter 14

Assessing Electoral Competition in Nigeria

The selection of public officials through elections that match two or more parties or candidates is electoral competition[1]. In functional democracies, opposition parties thrive; elections are free and fair; and ruling parties are sometimes voted out of power[2]. A democratic state espouses and supports such essential rights as freedom of expression, worship, movement, assembly, and from want[3]. More so the democratic state holds regular elections, supervised by independent and impartial electoral commissions[4].

A state or regime is not democratic by calling it so or by merely embracing such institutions of democracy as the legislature and judiciary, as is the case in electoral authoritarianism. Being democratic means welcoming the existence of opposition parties, and letting them organize and campaign freely against the ruling party. Being democratic means having the checks and balances that ensure political accountability, especially through genuine electoral competition. The greater checks on politicians and the greater accountability to citizens are both indicators by which a distinction can be made of democratic regimes from authoritarian regimes[5].

Democracy lives and is sustained by competition that requires that there be opposition parties offering voters potential alternative"[6]. Under the genuine electoral competitions, the citizens are able to pressure the major parties to be more accountable"[7]. Modern democratic theory essentially conceptualizes a democratic system as the polity that affords its citizen the opportunity to replace their political representation through regularly scheduled, competitive and open elections[8]. The assessment criteria for electoral competition in Nigeria will, therefore, be; the presence of credible opposition, competitiveness of elections, and openness of elections.

Presence of Credible Opposition

In *Political Man: The Social Bases on Politics,* Seymour Martin Lipset indicated that the existence of the opposition, is in essence, an alternative government; serving as a restraint on the incumbent government[9]. Only an opposition that has the potential to win an election and form a new government can provide a strong external incentive for the incumbent government to act in the interest of the citizens[10]. Political competition, when accompanied by repeated and genuine elections, therefore, generates a credible threat of this replacement[11].

Without the credible threat of replacements through elections, however, elected officials have fewer incentives to provide public goods. In ideal democratic settings, when incumbent governments sense that the opposition is strong and credible enough to take power, they act in ways that would enhance public satisfaction with their activities[12].

It is, therefore, the presence of credible opposition that ushers in accountability. This political accountability, arising from electoral competition, encourages the responsiveness of the elected officials to the governed; the transparency of government actions and services; and the accessibility of all to government programs, and services to be of primary concern to elected officials[13]. Welfare-enhancing public goods are, therefore, encouraged when governments are made to be responsive and accountable through genuine electoral competition.

Competitiveness of Elections

The competitiveness of elections is the extent to which executives are chosen through competitive elections[14]. This can also be seen as the extent to which prevailing mode of advancement gives a subordinate equal opportunities to be a superordinate[15]. The defining characteristic of democracy is the system in which high political offices and legislature get elected by means of contested elections in which the political competition is formatted in such a manner the reasonable uncertainties exist with regard to outcomes[16]. This democratic system loses its genuineness whenever the voting system is compromised. A genuine democracy preserves the integrity of the ballot by preventing its corruption.

Openness of Elections

The openness of elections refers to the extent that all politically active population has an opportunity to attain executive positions through a regulated process[17]. The political activities are hinged on law; becoming more open, and hence increasing the democratic consciousness[18]. For the credibility of the process, elections require openness and transparency. Without openness or transparency, therefore, no accountability is possible[19]. Ultimately, the major issue for any democratic system is whether or not elections give the people control over their governments[20].

Chapter 15

Assessing Presidential Leadership Performance in Nigeria

Although a distinction exists between leadership and governance, most studies obfuscate the distinction and use governance and leadership synonymously[1]. As earlier defined, leadership is that process which involves the influencing of the behavior and performance of subordinates and followers. On the other hand, governance is understood as the implementation, maintenance and administration of public policies or organizational structures. Thus governance could be viewed as the implementation of the visions of leadership. Conceptually, governance entails an orientation toward stability, whereas leadership orients toward innovation[2].

Although any particular operational definition of governance quality will likely be contested, the worldwide governance indicators, developed by Daniel Kaufmann, Aart Kraay, and Massimo Mastruzzi for the World Bank Policy department measure six governance indicators: (a) voice and accountability, (b) political stability and absence of violence, (c) government effectiveness, (d) regulatory quality, (e) rule of law, and (d) control of corruption[3].

Good leadership and governance culminate to the effective provision of political and public goods to the citizens[4].

Leadership is, however, situational, as the concepts that define leadership are culturally and environmentally specific. A bold initiative by some former African heads of governments in forming the African Leadership council led to the promulgation of Code of African Leadership (called Mombasa Declaration) for promoting better leadership. The council indicated that appropriate and attainable leadership for Africa includes delivery of state and individual security, the rule of law, good education, economic growth, and the protection of civil rights and the empowerment of the civil society[5].

The Ibrahim index of African leadership, developed by the Mo Ibrahim Foundation also has similar presidential leadership assessment criteria for African countries; and measures the delivery of public goods and services to citizens by government and non-state actors[6]. This index on African leadership assesses governance against 84 criteria. These criteria, divided in four broad groups, include the public safety and rule of law; participation and human rights; sustainable economic opportunity and human development.

These criteria, divided in four broad groups, include the safety and rule of law; participation and human rights; sustainable economic opportunity; and human development. The safety and rule of law components are on such issues as domestic political persecution, personal safety, property rights, accountability, corruption, and national security.

The participation and human rights components reflect such issues as political participation, freedom of association, press freedom, civil rights and liberties, and gender equality.

On the sustainable economic opportunity component, the issues considered include environmental and rural investment, infrastructure development, private sector involvement, across the border trading, and ease of obtaining licenses, access to credit, competitive environment, and economic management.

The human development component involves immunization, poverty, health, and education issues. This leadership index was, however, silent on the issue of corruption; but obviously, corruption is the bane of leadership and development in Nigeria.

A main function of political leadership is to provide public goods. Public goods are goods and services that are by their nature, necessary and available to everyone. The delivery of these public goods and services is the main thrust of public service. The presidential leadership performance indicators that are central to the development prospects of Nigeria are, therefore; the enhancement of public safety and rule of law, protection of political rights and civil liberties, creating sustainable economic opportunities through public policies, and control of corruption are crucial[7].

The indicators of presidential leadership performance in Nigeria would, therefore, be; protection of human rights, enthronement of rule of law, enhancing public safety, creating sustainable economic opportunities for the citizens, investment in human development and definite and concise efforts to control corruption.

Public Safety

Democracy starts with the citizens, with the pillars of the democratic framework embedded in the rights of the citizens and the ability of the state to guarantee equal rights of the citizens through constitutional and legal processes[8]. There can probably be little or no economic growth or development without the basic security[9]. The function of the state with respect to internal security is not only to enhance security by lowering crime rates, but also enable citizens to resolve their differences without resorting to arms or physical coercion. The delivery of the other public and political goods becomes more feasible only when reasonable provisions for public safety and security have been made and obtained.

Enthronement of Rule of Law

The next desirable political good is the provisions of predictable and systematic methods for dispute arbitration and adjudication, and for regulating the norms and values of the society[10]. The delivery of this political good, otherwise called the rule of law, demands enforceable body of laws, security of private property, enforceability of contracts, and effective judiciary[11]. This also entails the respect of the basic civil and human rights of all citizens, residents, and visitors within the geographical boundaries of the nation.

Where, as in all authoritarian regimes, power is, however, personalized, it becomes difficult to develop the legal and bureaucratic apparatuses of the state[12]. In Nigeria, even the usually slow judicial processes are usually subjected to political interferences[13]. As electoral authoritarian regimes, civilian presidents in Nigeria tend to adhere to a weak form of rule of law, in which governments regularly attempt to subordinate the judiciary. The judicial challenge in Nigeria is usually the contest between the rule of law and the rule of the ruling political elites; making the rule of law in Nigeria essentially the "rule of the jungle."

Protection of Civil and Human rights

The value of democracy lies on the protection of rights[14]. The rule of law, which guarantees the protection of the civil and human rights of citizens, is ensured through such watchdogs as independent and well-functioning judiciary and fearless and free press[15]. The protection of civil and human rights of the citizens is an essential public good and both of these watchdogs require protection from authoritarian leadership.

There have been arguments contending that the low literacy level in Nigeria makes it difficult for the citizens and civil societies to safeguard human rights in the society[16]. Granted that the awareness of civil rights is low and that the mass mobilization of the civil society is more tasking, the overarching challenge for a Nigerian president is whether civil and political rights are equally guaranteed for all.

Sustainable economic Opportunity

Another essential public good is the creation of enabling and conducive environments for economic development and prosperity at both the state and individual levels[17]. An open and accountable democratic system is more likely to provide greater opportunities for fostering and sustaining economic development[18]. Another challenge for Nigerian president whether economic rights are equally guaranteed for all. The presidential leadership assessors; namely; public safety, rule of law, civil rights, control of corruption control of corruption all associate positively with economic growth and human development in Nigeria[19].

Effectiveness of Governance

A responsive presidential leadership is more likely to provide greater opportunities that foster economic development by using the tools of public policy formulation and implementation. Incumbent Nigerian presidents usually claim their public policies are aimed at providing economic opportunities to the citizens. Whether or not these government policies actually provide economic opportunities for citizens could be more thoroughly analyzed by assessing the effectiveness of bureaucratic governance. Assessing the effectiveness of the federal bureaucracy will be more precise and accurate in determining the level of government commitment toward providing the environments for economic development in the country; and for the citizens.

Control of Corruption

The World Bank identifies corruption as the greatest obstacle to development because it distorts the rule of law and weakens the foundations of public institutions[20]. The International Monetary Fund (IMF) has also determined that countries with high corruption levels have less of their GPD going into investment[21]. Corruption, in slowing down economic development, stifles productive investment and escalates the cost of business, as well as the cost of public projects. These vices are capable of repressing economic development and productivity. The problem of corruption in Nigeria extends through all layers of bureaucracy, including customs, police and the security and defence organs of the government[22]. Although a weak rule of law reigns within the country, the lack of the political will to control corruption and the non-enforcement of regulations remain major problems.

Human Development

Development occurs when a nation acquires the social, economic, political and technological wherewithal to understand the laws of nature and its environment, and uses that to attain the capacities that enable it meet the needs of its citizens[23]. Development can also be considered as the process of transforming social, economic, and political system into their modern states[24]. In politics, the modern governmental system must exhibit high levels of differentiation and functional specialization in governance[25].

The essence of development is not only industrialization, but also of changes in attitudes, social values, and lifestyles[26]. Development is inherently beneficial to societies and must be promoted through the suppression or removal of any obstacles. Currently, the UNDP indicates that the emphasis is on human development; with leading a long and healthy life (life expectancy), being knowledgeable (educational attainment), and decent standard of living (income per capita) as the basic indicators[27].

Chapter 16

Electoral Competition and Presidential Leadership Performance: A Research Study on Nigeria

In my doctorate dissertation research on "Electoral Competition and Presidential Leadership Performance in Nigeria", I determined and explained the relationships that exist between the job performance of a democratic president and the quality of electoral competition in the country. The research study pinpointed correlations that are not only enormously significant but are also related to the question of whether improvement in electoral competition could be a major pathway to the improvement in presidential leadership performance in Nigeria, thereby hastening the development of the country.

The primary research goal was to investigate how electoral competition relates to the performance of presidential leadership, thereby becoming an effective tool toward improving the living conditions of Nigerians. I measured the presidential leadership performance in Nigeria against such meaningful benchmarks as the provision of public safety and rule of law, protection of human rights, effectiveness of governance, control of corruption, and human development in the country.

The result of the multiple regressions, the t-tests of difference of means of the dependent variables, and hypotheses testing, offered sufficient reasons to conclude that presidential leadership performance, enhanced through genuine electoral competition, is crucial for the development of Nigeria. The potential political and social change significance of this study is that it showed that the better the electoral competition becomes, the more the positive spillover effects will have on the entire political leadership performance in Nigeria.

The emerging evidence from the study was found consistent with such existing concepts as the relationship of electoral competition to responsiveness and accountability, quality of governance, political stability, human rights protection, and encouragement of credible opposition[1].

In a democracy, electoral competition creates incentives for elected presidents to be responsive and accountable to the electorates. Genuine electoral competition is, therefore, more likely to increase presidential leadership performance than a situation in which the selection of a candidate is not based on competition or in which the competition has been compromised through electoral manipulations and rigging.

The primary conclusion of study is that the absence of or minimal electoral competition creates poor presidential leadership performance that impedes the development of Nigeria. This rested on the reasoning that, whenever electoral competition is compromised or restricted, Nigerian presidents do not have incentives to improve on their leadership performance. Another perspective of the study was that this poor presidential leadership performance affects national development because it does not create incentives for the elected president to deliver on public goods.

From the statistical outcome of the test results, the null hypothesis that there are no differences in the mean of the protection of human rights, effectiveness of governance, and human development in the presidential leadership years with electoral competition and the presidential leadership years without electoral competition was rejected. These results provided statistical evidence to show that the protection of human rights, effectiveness of governance, and human development are greater in the presidential leadership years with electoral competition than those years without or with less electoral competition.

The study results also verified the theoretical framework that predicted correlation between electoral competition and such presidential leadership performance indicators as public safety and rule of law, protection of human rights, effectiveness of governance, control of corruption, and human development. The analysis, however, showed that only the protection of human rights, control of corruption, effectiveness of governance, and human development are statistically significant. There is, therefore, evidence to conclude that electoral competition is positively related to protection of human rights, control of corruption, effectiveness of governance, and human development in Nigeria[2].

With the protection of human rights, effectiveness of governance, control of corruption, and human development positively correlated with both openness and competitiveness of election and presence of credible opposition, similar outcomes might be expected if genuine electoral competition becomes part of the political and electoral reform policy in Nigeria, which is expected to correlate to increased responsiveness to citizens' needs.

From the outcome of the research, the study concluded that based on measurable empirical results, the greater the level of electoral competition in Nigeria, the more improved the presidential leadership performance.

Essentially, the study showed that increased understanding of these factors will affect positive social change through the recommendation for improvements in the presidential leadership performance as indicated by: (a) improvement in public safety and rule of law; (b) protection of human rights; (c) effectiveness of governance; and (d) control of corruption; and (e) improvement in human development indicators, namely increased literacy, longer life expectancy, and a higher standard of living.

The results of this research underscore as well as amplify the need for Nigeria to undergo political transition by consolidating its democracy. The political transition refers to the stage in political development when a state transits from authoritarian to democratic system of governance. In the book, *Financial Globalization and Democracy in Emerging Markets,* Leslie Elliott Armijo "described the democratization process as a trajectory pathway of political liberalization (loosening the overt controls of authoritarianism), formal and official transition to democracy, and then democratic consolidation[3]. The last component of consolidation involves the normative acceptance and internalization of the new democratic procedures and processes by the major political participants. Leslie Armijo argued that "the problem with the regimes in the developing countries is that they are 'stuck' between the formal transition to democracy and the democratic consolidation stage[4]. The transition paradigm therefore makes the assumption that any country moving away from authoritarian rule is in transition, in as much as elections are the determinants of who wields elective political power[5]. Such countries like Nigeria are not even in transition to democracy, but are rather in a state of normality[6].

This transition is most relevant because democracy, which is an important component of free government, carries certain risks, which if not checked, could bring about tyranny and domination[7]. Such risks include the absence of genuine electoral competition, which has transformed most of the civilian regimes in Nigeria into electoral dictatorship. Obviously, as earlier indicated, the consolidation of democracy occurs only after two electoral turnovers with the party in power at beginning of the transition losing a subsequent election, turning over power to the opposition, and the new incumbents losing power to another party in a subsequent election[8].

Essentially, a political leadership performance quality that is important to the development prospects of Nigeria relates to the open and transparent conduct of free and fair elections that would lead to improvements in such governance quality dimension as the provision of public safety and rule of law, protection of human rights, effectiveness of governance, control of corruption, and human development in the country. Genuine electoral competition generated by the process and consolidation of democracy can be effective in improving the performances of political leadership in Nigeria.

Although the study sought to investigate the relationship of electoral competition and presidential

leadership performance, it nonetheless, found peculiar problems with Nigeria's political system, namely:
(i) Practices of electoral authoritarianism.
(ii) Minimal openness and competitiveness in elections
(iii) No uncertainty of outcome in presidential elections
(iv) Nigerian presidents manipulate elections through bribery of electoral and security officials.
(v) Rather than improving governance, incumbent presidents bribe and hijack electoral processes.
(vi) Nigerian presidents do not have electoral incentives to improve on leadership performances.
(vii) Resources for development is diverted toward influencing the electoral processes and outcomes.
(viii) Opposition parties are systematically disadvantaged
(ix) The presidents perform poorly, but citizens are rendered incapable of voting them out.
(x)Voting citizens are rendered inconsequential to presidents' stay in power.
(xii) Presidents become unaccountable to electorate.
(xiii) Quality of presidential leadership is, therefore, compromised.

The study also achieved significant outcomes by:
(i) Creating more understanding of the electoral practices that have undermined the performance of Nigeria's presidents.
(ii) Increasing the possibilities for addressing the prevailing problem of poor presidential leadership performance in Nigeria
(iii) Making recommendations that could provide the platform for much-needed changes in the electoral processes and development of Nigeria.

(iv) Pinpointing correlations that show genuine electoral competition as a major pathway to the desired improvements in presidential leadership performance.
(v) Providing the understanding that some factors that could lead to improved lives for Nigerian citizens go hand-in-hand with the existence of genuine competition among parties or candidates for presidential elections.

PART VII

Nigeria: Prospects for Reforms

Chapter 17

Enthronement of Genuine Electoral Competition

As Robert Dahl indicated in *Polyarchy*, the constructs of democracy assume that the voters' preferences are respected[1]. The key concepts of democracy are meant to ensure, among others things, the integrity of electoral competition. In democratic regimes, therefore, such practices as free and fair elections and freedom of association are used to ensure effective political participation and competition[2]. The competition for elective position is, moreover, necessary because the preference of rulers and the ruled may sometimes be divergent[3].

The competition inherent in democratic elections is a tool by which the citizens pressure the elected officials to be accountable to the electorates. From the liberal democratic theory, accountability of the government can be achieved through recurrent elections[4]. The conducts of elections, it must be understood, do not mean that the country is a democracy.

Electoral competition which is, hinged on fair and open elections in which the performances of the elected official are subjected to the ultimate evaluation is of utmost importance to the success or failure of a democracy[5]. A "free" election can be conceptualized as one in which voters openly express their preferences and political parties are unhindered; whereas a "fair" election entails that rules and the processes of the elections are impartial[6].

Electoral competition should, therefore, be analyzed from the perspectives of its ultimate intentions, which is, reflection of voters' preferences and participation[7]. These two characteristics, generated by first-order competition are describable as genuine electoral competition[8]. This theory of genuine electoral competition therefore shifts the focus from what-groups-get-what from the representation to a new normative focus on the quality of electoral competition among leaders[9].

In an expanded format, the three processes of electoral competition are; issue identification, participation, and election. The identification of policy issues and public problems are important in electoral competition because the feelings and opinion of the citizenry in identifying the public problems to act upon is crucial. Participation empowers the citizens through their active participation; and hence their ability to elect or dismiss their political leaders by means of genuine competitive elections. The third processes are meaningful, fair, and open elections in which officials and their performances are subjected to the ultimate contests.

Electoral competition, therefore, creates and guarantees accountability, imposes constraints on executive arbitrariness, and improves representation, and participation. Moreover, the tendency to convert public resources is discouraged when governments are made more politically responsive and accountable. Likewise, welfare-enhancing public goods are encouraged when governments are pressured to be responsive and accountable.

As is in many countries in Sub-Saharan Africa, electoral competition in Nigeria is minimal because, rather than improve their governance, most incumbent governments would rather devise more dubious means to hijack the electoral processes. In addition, the opposition in Nigeria is systematically disadvantaged; the citizens thus denied the power of checking government behaviors, and the quality of leadership. Losing the influence of their votes, and hence no influence over election outcomes, the entire citizenry becomes largely disadvantaged; and democracy loses its value.

Such indicators as presence of credible opposition, openness of elections, and competitiveness of elections could be operationalized as the measures of the level of electoral competition in Nigeria. To meet the criteria for genuine electoral competition, the electoral process must be genuinely free and fair, respecting the sovereignty, and electoral desires of the people. Obviously, the fundamental difference in disposition and performance among democratic regimes are reflections of the differences in quality of electoral competition.

Chapter 18

Enthronement of Developmental Leadership

Leadership is the most critical factor in giving the required impetus to nations, social, and political movements[1]. Leadership can also be seen as a form of power in which the wielders compete with others, using the resources available to them to influence others toward the attainment of set goals[2]. Although leadership involves that use of power, the exercise of power itself is not leadership[3]. Power is not the act of changing the attitude and behavior of others, but rather the potential to do so[4].

Power, when well used, is usually geared toward uplifting the welfare of the citizens. The practice of leadership, therefore, forms an integral part of the development of states and nations. Democratic leadership offers great promise for nation-building, socio-political stability, peace and respect for human dignity. Creating effective leadership, however, requires the enthronement of the rule of law, ensuring freedom of speech, association and the press, and fighting corruption.

Leadership can also be described as a system of interacting inputs, processes, outputs, and feedback that desire meaningful direction and purpose from the performance system and environment within which leadership occurs[5]. The phenomenon of leadership, therefore, comes with the need to achieve the goals desired by the internal and external stakeholders of a specific performance system such as a nation[6]. Leadership requires communicating goals, roles, and responsibilities inspiring confidence in leadership direction and resources, resolving issues, and delivering results[7]. Leadership conceptualizes the future, aligns goals with the common vision, and provides the inspirations needed to achieve transformational goals[8]. These perspectives give credence to the situational theory of leadership.

Leaders with strong people-oriented styles would listen to followers, do personal favors to followers and support their interest when require, and treat them as equals[9]. On followership, well informed and confident followers would most likely prefer participative or achievement-oriented leadership; whereas ill-informed followers or those that lack self-confidence are more likely to embrace supportive or directive leadership[10]. Effective leaders, therefore, strengthen the effort-to-performance expectancy by ensuring that followers have the information, support, and the resources they need to perform their duties[11]. The performance of the leader is, hence, enhanced as the readiness level of the followers increase. Increasing leadership behavior from the lower level of providing instructions; to selling and explaining; to followers' participation; and then to delegating responsibilities, would gradually increase the readiness level of the followers.

Fred Fiedler, in his contingency model of leadership, argued that leadership is dependent on the complex situation by which the leader operates; including the nature of the situation, environment and subordinates[12]. Leadership should be analyzed from the ability to influence action and motivation based on situational contexts and follower characteristics[13]. Obviously, human efforts are needed to align individual traits to the environment. Invariably, personality and situational factors interact in determining whether or not a person will rise to leadership[14].

As leaders must adapt to the environment and to be judged effective, political leadership performances in Nigeria must be evaluated against such meaningful benchmarks as the provision of public safety and rule of law, protection of human rights, creation of sustainable economic opportunities for the citizens, control of corruption and improvement in the living standards of the citizens.

Chapter 19

Curbing corruption: The Curse of Underdevelopment

United Nations Development Program (UNDP) defines corruption as the abuse of power for private benefit through bribery, extortion, influence peddling, nepotism, fraud, or embezzlement[1]. Corruption does not only undermine investment and economic growth, it also aggravates poverty as even the poor have to bribe to obtain basic services in Nigeria. Nigeria still stands as an example of an African country whose development has stalled because of corruption. The corruption-prone and compromised public institutions share a large portion of the blame for the disappointing economic performances and poor developmental strategies that have continued to bestride the country.

The business elites collude with the bureaucratic and political elites to embezzle from the national treasury for personal use; thereby, undermining the accumulation of financial resources needed for the development of welfare-enhancing projects. This corruption has had adverse effects on national development as it stalls economic activities and development; and deters productive investment as resources are likely to flow out to other countries in which the investment climates are more favorable.

Moreover, a state in which corruption and patrimonial leadership are prevalent would suffer in relations to modernization because the personalized distributions of state resources to cronies are usually leveraged over the welfare-enhancing public goods and services. Generally, any country that is characterized by widespread personalization of power and massive corruption is not likely to experience modernization[2].

With corruption, good governance and development suffer; ethnic, religious, and political conflicts intensify; and the citizens begin to pray for the return authoritarian military regimes[3]. Obviously, the cost of defecting from democracy would be too great as it would permit the return to authoritarianism.

The major impediments to curbing corruption in Nigeria include the low risk of detection and punishment; the absence of unified national value-system, and the lack of political will to curb corruption. By virtue of the differentials in culture and religion; and hence the absence of unified national value, different segments of the population perceive corruption differently. Meaningful fights against corruption have always assumed ethnic configuration and biases.

The lacking commitment of political leaders to the eradication of corruption, is another impediment on the fight against corruption. Corruption in Nigeria is essentially a conspiracy of the elites. Rather than invest the mineral resource revenues into infrastructure and education, Nigerian leaders, often, in collusion with exploration companies, siphon proceeds from the country's resources into their own pockets. Nigerian elites are not outraged or embarrassed by the level of corruption in the country. Rather, they bide their time, position themselves, and wait for own opportunities for corrupt enrichment.

Corruption in Nigeria can be curbed if political leaders are willing to impartially embark on such anti-corruption strategies as reducing and streamlining regulations to reduce opportunities for corruption; as well as increasing the potentials for detecting and punishing corrupt officials. A number of countries in Asia that earlier had similar corruption issues as Nigeria have been able to curb corruption by adopting policies that reduced bureaucracy; and have reinforced the detection and sanctioning capacities of anti-corruption agencies in their countries.

Chapter 20

Prospects for Exemplary Leadership

As any particular operational definition of governance quality is bound to be contestable, some indicators that have been used to operationalize the quality of governance include economic policy coherence, public service effectiveness, and limited corruption[1]. The indicators of ethical governance would include placing emphasis on establishing a clean and honest civil service; strong anti-corruption measures; emphasis on accountability and transparency; and accepting media scrutiny on the government[2].

Obviously, national development is influenced largely by political considerations, with good political governance been a prerequisite for good economic governance and national development[3]. In Nigeria, many attempts at building a functioning and stable democratic state has continually failed due to poor leadership. Obviously, genuine democratic institutions will promote developmental governance by countering those corrupt behaviors that cause economic damage to the country. Moreover, the antidote to the political opportunism that is prevalent in Nigeria is to force the Nigerian political leaders to internalize the cost of this behavior by making governments accountable to the citizenry through elections that allow free and fair competition.

In the past, ninety percent of African nations have experienced despotic rulers, who rather than using power for public goods, used the power as an end in itself. Africa has, therefore, been long saddled with various forms of poor and malevolent leaderships, manned by *kleptocrats*, economic illiterates, and military-installed autocrats; with the most egregious leaders coming from Nigeria, Democratic republic of Congo and Zimbabwe, in spite of the abundance of natural resources in these countries[4]. Under the leadership of these despots, infrastructures degenerated into despair; while healthcare, educational standards and life expectancy declined[5]. Obviously, the much needed public funds for the needed socio-economic infrastructures are constantly and systematically siphoned and hidden in local and foreign bank accounts.

There are, however, few well-established democracies in Sub-Saharan Africa, accepting the separation of power, and institutionalized checks and balances[6]. Such countries are known to follow written constitutional mandates; supporting the independence of judiciary, permitting parliamentary checks, and preventing the executive head from exercising unlimited power[7]. These genuinely democratic countries encourage a culture of accountability, freedom of expression and free press, and a tolerance for dissent[8]. Typical examples of such well-established democratic countries that usually deliver the most and best quality public goods are Botswana and Mauritius.

Fortunately, these few examples of good leadership stand out by their strength of character and adherence to the principles of democracy. The successes of Botswana and Mauritius are somewhat deeply rooted in the unwavering democratic dispositions of their founding leaders, namely Seretsekharma of Botswana and Seewoosagur Ramgoolan[9]. These leaders could have joined their contemporaries in imposing iron-handed one-man kleptomaniac rule on their countrymen and women; but they did not. Botswana is, hence, one country that seems to have escaped the "resource" curse of some other African countries[10]. In terms of democracy, stability, and rapid growth of income, Botswana stands out as one of the best in Africa[11].

Likewise, the visionary and effective leadership of Nelson Mandela was decisive in helping South Africa evolve into a functional and development-oriented democratic state rather than a post-apartheid fractured and autocratic state [12]. Other countries that seem to be showing promise by following the exemplary leadership of these countries include Ghana and Lesotho.

Chapter 21

National Reform Agenda

Elections must reflect will of Electorates

A state or regime is democratic, not by calling it so or by merely embracing such institutions of democracy as legislature and judiciary; but rather largely on the conduct of free and fair elections that reflect the wishes of the electorate. The constructs of modern democracy must, therefore, be attentive to the system through which people compete for votes[1].

Specifically, modern democratic theory conceptualizes a democratic system as the polity that affords its citizen the opportunity to replace their political representation through regularly scheduled, competitive and open elections[2]. This potential and capacity of the electorate to elect or dismiss the government through established electoral procedures are therefore conditions for accountability[3].

Democratic governance not only recognizes, but also institutionalizes the people as the fountain of power; enabling them, by means of intervaled-elections, to choose and mandate those to govern[4]. To enhance political leadership performance, the electoral process must be made genuinely democratic; respecting and accepting the sovereignty and electoral desires of the people. More so, being an electoral democracy means that the electoral process is protected as to ensure that elections reflect the will of the electorates.

Establishing an Electoral Trust Council

The concept separation of power entails the existence of the executive, legislative, and judiciary arms of government. Of these three arms, only the executive and legislative arms are subjected to periodic elections in Nigeria. Achieving impartiality in the electoral process becomes more challenging when any of the executive or legislative arms is involved in the selection or appointment of election officials.

A way to overcome this challenge is to set up an Electoral Trust Council (ETC) consisting of all the retired judges of the federal appeal courts and supreme courts who are still below the age of 80years. Judges have never been subjected to elections, and are therefore expected to remain non-partisan. This establishment of the ETC would create a good measure of stability as its membership will run on a stable progression of retired judges. This body will replace the current functions of the executive and legislature in appointing the federal and state electoral commissioners; making the appointments less partisan and more impartial. The council's deliberations could be in secrecy and under the oath of disclosure, except for announced decisions.

Similarly, the same concept of the ETC could be replicated at the state level with the membership of the council consisting of all retired high court judges, below the age of 75, in each state. The state ETC would appoint the state electoral commissioner and the returning officers in the local government areas.

Essentially, the executive and legislative control over

the appointments of top electoral officials is an implicit conflict of interest that undermines the impartiality and genuineness of the electoral process. An actionable solution would, hence, be to institute these truly independent trust councils. This would insulate the electoral processes from the abuses of elected officials whose primary interest is not to nurture democracy but rather to perpetuate themselves or cronies in power.

Refocusing the International Monitoring of Elections

The international electoral monitoring agencies must always take into account; the underlying issues and logics of politics in Nigeria, especially, the penchant of political officeholders to abuse the electoral process; repress the opposition; rig elections; and barricade themselves in power. If Nigeria has to become genuinely democratic, the international monitoring agencies as well as international development assistance agencies must target the way politics works in the country, especially its predatory nature[5].

To reform the electoral process to ensure free and fair elections, there will be need for international observer organizations to constantly invoke and promote a wider use of international law as it strengthens genuine elections. The United Nations General Assembly in resolution 16/163 acknowledges the importance of international election observation for the promotion of free and fair election and its contribution toward enhancing the integrity of the election processes[6]. There is strong evidence to inform the necessity for international development and donor organizations to insist on the reform of the electoral system to reflect the true intentions of the voting citizens as conditions for project financing and donor assistance.

In conjunction with all stakeholders, especially opposition parties, international election observers should be specific about the criteria, procedures, and benchmarks for genuine elections as conditions for participating and vetting particular elections. The strict adherence to these criteria should form the basis for declaring an election as free and fair, or not.

Reforming Public Institutions

The quality public institutions are deep fundamental factors that determine which countries experience good performance and which do not[7]. The quality of institutions and governance are major determinants of whether or not natural resources could be a curse to long-term development[8]. For instance, in considering the so-called resource curse, it is obvious that the oil is not necessarily the cause; but rather, when a country already has good institutions at the time the mineral resource is discovered, the country is more likely to put the oil to use for national welfare instead of elites' welfare. An urgent need exists for reforming and strengthening public institutions in Nigeria.

Transparency and Accountability

Democracy bears some time-cherished values as equality of citizenry, the responsiveness and accountability of the government to the governed, the transparency of government actions and services, and the accessibility of government programs and services to all; which, have over the decades, evolved from democratic governance. The United Nations General Assembly resolution 59/201 indicates that accountability and transparency in public administration and public affairs is an essential element of democracy[9]. Accountability requires that the citizens using the instruments of the media, elections, legislature, courts, or other independent institutions should be able to hold those in power responsible for their actions[10].

Generally, accountability requires a high degree of transparency, which, refers to unfettered access by the public to timely and reliable on the decisions and performance of the public sector[11]. Political activities should be geared toward accountability that is hinged on law; as well as on open and transparent processes[12]. This accountability ensures the responsiveness and accountability of the government to the governed, as well as the transparency of government actions and services.

The public demand for accountability creates incentives for governments to adopt policies conducive to growth[13]. By compelling elected officials to consider the electoral consequences of their actions and inactions, democratic accountability increases the chances of delivering public goods. The tendency to convert public resources is also discouraged when governments are made more politically responsive and accountable; as likewise, the encouragement of welfare-enhancing public goods.

Control of Corruption

The most profound challenge to democracy in Nigeria is the control of corruption. Corruption builds up situations where public officials serve their own ends rather than public good; and public resources are cornered into private pockets. Corruption in Nigeria is endemic and inhibits the desired outcomes of democracy and development.

For democracy to be sustainable, Nigeria's political leaders must demonstrate that they are meeting the citizens' expectation of better life, freedom, justice, and good governance. These leaders must work better to contain crime and corruption, generate economic growth, secure justice; otherwise the people will lose faith in democracy and clamour for alternative forms of governance[14].

The fight against bureaucratic corruption may start with the enactment of such strong anti-corruption legislations that ae similar to those for Hong Kong[15]:

"(1) Any person who, whether in Nigeria or elsewhere, without lawful authority or reasonable excuse, offers any advantage to a public servant as an inducement to or reward for or otherwise on account of that public servant's-(a) performing or abstaining from performing, or having performed or abstained from performing , any act in his/her capacity as a public servant; (b) expediting, delaying, hindering or preventing, or having expedited, delayed, hindered, or prevented, the performance of an act, whether by that public servant, or by any other public servant in his or that other public servant's capacity as a public servant; or (c) assisting, favouring, hindering or delaying, or having assisted, favoured, hindered or delayed, any person in the transaction of any business with a public body, shall be guilty of an offence.

(2) Any public servant who, whether in Nigeria or elsewhere, without lawful authority or reasonable excuse, solicits or accepts any advantage as an inducement to or reward for or otherwise on account of his-(a) performing of abstaining from performing, or having performed or abstained from performing, any act in his capacity as a public servant; (b) expediting, delaying, hindering or preventing, or having expedited, delayed, hindered, or prevented, the performance of an act, whether by himself,

or by any other public servant in his or that other public servant's capacity as a public servant; or (c) assisting, favouring, hindering or delaying, or having assisted, favoured, hindered or delayed, any person in the transaction of any business with a public body, shall be guilty of an offence".

The fight against other public and political corruption requires an independent anti-corruption agency fortified with such legislation as following:

"(1) Any person who, being or having been a prescribed public officer or political office-holder-(a) maintains a standard of living above which is not commensurate with his present or past official emoluments; or (b) is in control of pecuniary resources or property disproportionate to his present or past official emoluments, shall, unless he gives a satisfactory explanation to the court as to how he was able to maintain such a standard of living or how such pecuniary resources or property came under his control, be guilty of an offence"[16].

For Nigeria to achieve sustainable development, the democratic practices must become accountable and responsive; working better to control corruption and constrain the abuse of power, so that the main responsibility of elected officials becomes the delivery of public good rather than private good.

NOTES

Preface
1. McFerson, H. M. (2009). Governance and hyper-corruption in resource-rich African countries. *Third World Quarterly, 30(8),* 1529-1548, p.1540.
2. Rotberg, R. (2007). *Governance and leadership in Africa*, Broomal, PA: Mason Crest Publishers.
3. Alence, R. (2004). Political institutions and development governance in Sub-Saharan Africa. *Journal of Modern African Studies, 42* (2), 163-187.
4. Ibid.
5. Rotberg, R. (2007). *Governance and leadership in Africa*, Broomal, PA: Mason Crest Publishers.

Introduction: Nigeria: Historical and Political Perspectives
1. Central Intelligence Agency (CIA). 2009. *The World fact book: Nigeria.* http://www.cia.gov/cia/publications/factbook/geos/ni.html.
2. Schraeder, P.J. (2004). *African politics and society: A mosaic in transformation*. New York: Thomson Belmont.
3. Ibid
4. Ibid
5. Adamolekun, L. (1998).*Politics and Administration in Nigeria*. London: Spectrum Books.
6. Preston, L.E. & Post, J.E. (1975). *Private Management and Public Policy: The Principle of Public Responsibility.* Englewood Cliffs, NJ: Prentice-Hall.

Chapter 1: The Spectrum of Political Systems of Governance
1. Marshall, M.G & Cole, B.R. (2009). *Global report 2009.*Severn, MD: Center for systemic Peace.
2. Ibid.
3. Ibid, p. 9).
4. Ibid, p.9).
5. Ibid.
6. Vestal, T.M. (1999). *Ethiopia: A Post-Cold War African State.* Westport, CT: Praeger Publishers.
7. Altemeyer, B. (1998). *The Authoritarian Specter.* Cambridge, MA: Harvard University Press.
8. Ekman, J. (2009). Political participation and regime stability: A framework for analyzing hybrid regimes. *International Political Science Review. 30* (1), 7-31.
9. Vestal, T.M. (1999). *Ethiopia: A Post-Cold War African State.* Westport, CT: Praeger Publishers.
10. Ekman, J. (2009). Political participation and regime stability: A framework for analyzing hybrid regimes. *International Political Science Review. 30* (1), 7-31.
11. Vestal, T.M. (1999). *Ethiopia: A Post-Cold War African State.* Westport, CT: Praeger Publishers.
12. Gerring, J., Philip, B., Barndt, W. T. & Moreno, C. (2005). Democracy and economic growth: A historical perspective. *World Politics, 57*, 323-264, P.333.
13. LeVan, A. (2007). *Dictators, democrats and development in Nigeria. A PhD*

Dissertation, University of California, San Diego. AAT 3283913.

14. Ibid.

15. Schumpeter, J. (1947). *Capitalism, socialism and democracy.* London: George Allen and Unwin, p. 269.

16. Lipset, S. M. (1963). *Political Man: The social bases of politics.* Garden City, NY: Double day & Company. p. 71.

17. Huntington, S.P. (1993). The Third Wave: Democratization in the Late 20th Century. Norman, OK: University of Oklahoma Press. p.195.

18. International IDEA (2008). *Assessing the quality of democracy: An overview of the international IDEA framework.* Stockholm: International IDEA.

19. USAID Policy (1991). Democracy and Governance. Washington, DC.

20. Shafritz, J.M., Russell, E.W. & Borick, C.P. (2007). *Introducing Public Administration.* 5[th]Ed.New York: Pearson-Longman.

21. International IDEA (2008). *Assessing the quality of democracy: An overview of the international IDEA framework.* Stockholm: International IDEA.

22. Satyanath, S. & Subramanian, A. (2004). What determines long-run macroeconomic stability? *IMF Working paper No 04/215.* Retrieved from social science electronic Publishing, Inc.

Chapter 2: Democracy: Classical Theories and Constructs

1. Bowman, K.S. (1996). Taming the Tiger: Militarization and Democracy in Latin America. *Journal of Peace Research,* Volume *33 (3):* 289-308.

2. USAID Policy (1991). Democracy and Governance. Washington, DC

3. Freeman, S. (2000) Deliberative Democracy: A Sympathetic Comment. *Philosophy and Public Affairs,* Volume *29* (4), p.371.

4. Cremona, R.K. (2006). *A meaningful majority: Rediscovering government by the people.* Ph.D. Dissertation. State University of New York New York, United States, ATT 3220350.

5. Foweraker, J. & Krznaric, R. (2001). How to construct a database of liberal democratic performance. *Democratization, 8*(3), 1-25.

6. Dahl, R. A. (1956). *A preface to democratic theory.* Chicago, IL: The University of Chicago Press.

7. Lipstz, K. L. (2004). *Campaigns and competition: How to enhance voter knowledge* and deliberation in mass democracy. Ph.D. Dissertation. University of California. Berkley, United States, AAT 3167206.

8. Schumpeter, J. (1947). *Capitalism, socialism and democracy.* London: George Allen and Unwin.

9. Lipstz, K. L. (2004). *Campaigns and competition: How to enhance voter knowledge* and deliberation in mass democracy. Ph.D. Dissertation. University of California. Berkley, United States, AAT 3167206.

10. Ibid.

11. Dahl, R. A. (1989). *Democracy and its critics.* New Haven, CT: Yale University Press.

12. Lipstz, K. L. (2004). *Campaigns and competition: How to enhance voter knowledge* and deliberation in mass democracy. Ph.D. Dissertation. University of

California. Berkley, United States (Publication Number AAT 3167206).
13. Ibid.
14. Ibid.
15. Ibid.
16. Ibid.
17. Gomez-Albarello, J.G. (2006). *From an impartial vantage point from democratic theory to theory of action and vice versa.* Ph.D. Dissertation. Washington University. Washington, United States, AAT3238650.

Chapter 3: Democracy: Contemporary Theories and Constructs
1. Robinson, W. (2007). Democracy or Polyarchy? *NACLA Report on the Americas.* Vol. 40 (1).
2. Ibid.
3. Schemeil, Y. (2000). Democracy before Democracy. *International Political Science Review*, Volume *21* (2): 99-120.
4. Dahl, R. A. (1971). *Polyarchy.* New Haven, CT: Yale University Press.
5. Dahl, R. A. (1956). *A preface to democratic theory.* Chicago, IL: The University of Chicago Press.
6. Dahl, R. A. (1971). *Polyarchy.* New Haven, CT: Yale University Press.
7. Coppedge, M. (2007). In Defense of Polyarchy. *NACLA Report on the Americas.* Volume *40* (1).
8. Ibid.
9. Raskin, J.B. (2003). *Overriding Democracy: The Supreme Court Vs the American*
10. Schemeil, Y. (2000). Democracy before Democracy. *International Political Science Review*, Volume *21* (2): 99-120.
11. Ibid.
12. Ibid.
13. Ibid.
14. Manin, B. (1997). *The Principles of Representative Government.* Uk: Cambridge University Press.
15. Goebel, T. (2002). *Direct Democracy in America 1800-1940:A government by the People.* Chapel Hill, NC: University of North Carolina Press.
16. Roberts, N. (2004). Public Deliberation in an Age of Direct Citizen Participation. *American Review of Public Administration,* Volume *34* (4) pp.315-353.
17. Ibid
18. Dahl, R. A. (1989). *Democracy and its critics.* New Haven, CT: Yale University Press.
19. Goebel, T. (2002). *Direct Democracy in America 1800-1940:A government by the People.* Chapel Hill, NC: University of North Carolina Press.
20. Marshall, M.G & Cole, B.R. (2009). *Global report 2009.* Severn, MD: Center for systemic Peace, p.9.
21. Ekman, J. (2009). Political participation and regime stability: A framework for analyzing hybrid regimes. *International Political Science Review.* *30* (1), 7-31.

22. Ibid.
23. Levitsky, S. & Way, L.A. (2002). The Rise of Competitive Authoritarianism. *Journal of Democracy,* Volume *13* (2): 51-65.

Chapter 4: Concepts of Genuine Democracy
1. International IDEA (2008). *Assessing the quality of democracy: An overview of the international IDEA framework.* Stockholm: International IDEA..
2. Marshall, M.G & Cole, B.R. (2009). *Global report 2009*.Severn, MD: Center for systemic Peace, p.9.
3. Ibid, p.10.
4. Ibid.
5. Diamond, L. (2008) *The Spirit of Democracy: The struggle to build free Societies throughout the World.* New York: Henry Holt.
6. International IDEA (2008). *Assessing the quality of democracy: An overview of the international IDEA framework.* Stockholm: International IDEA, p.17.
7. Ibid, p.17)
8. Diamond, L. (2008) *The Spirit of Democracy: The struggle to build free Societies throughout the World.* New York: Henry Holt.
9. Ibid.
10. Ibid.
11. Gerring, J., Philip, B., Barndt, W. T. & Moreno, C. (2005). Democracy and economic growth: A historical perspective. *World Politics, 57*, 323-264.
12. Maynor, J. (2006). Modern republican democratic contestation: A model of deliberative democracy. In I. Honohan & J. Jennings, *Republicanism in Theory and practice, 125*-139. NY: Rout ledge.
13. Wright, J. (2008). Political competition and democratic stability in new democracies. *B.J. Pol. S., 38*, 221-245.
14. Dahl, R. A. (1966). *Political opposition in Western democracies.* New Haven, CT: Yale University Press.
15. Diamond, L. (2008) *The Spirit of Democracy: The struggle to build free Societies throughout the World.* New York: Henry Holt.
16. Ibid, p. 25).
17. Ibid, p. 26).
18. Ibid.
19. Ibid
20. United Nations (2011).General Assembly Sixty-sixth Session: Strengthening the role of the United Nations in enhancing periodic and genuine elections and the promotion of democratization. Resolution No A/RES/66/163.
21. Huntington, S.P. (1993). The Third Wave: Democratization in the Late 20th Century. Norman, OK: University of Oklahoma Press.

Chapter 5: Sovereignty of the People: The core of Democratic Governance
1. Foweraker, J. & Krznaric, R. (2001). How to construct a database of liberal democratic performance. *Democratization, 8*(3), 1-25.
2. Rotberg, R. (2007). *Governance and leadership in Africa*, Broomal, PA: Mason

Crest Publishers.

3. Ibid.

4. Ibid.

5. Ibid.

6. UDHR (1948) Universal Declaration of Human Rights, United Nations.

7. LeVan, A. (2007). *Dictators, democrats and development in Nigeria. A PhD Dissertation,* University of California, San Diego. AAT 3283913.

8. Ibid.

9. Lake, D. & Baum, M. (2001).The Invisible hand of Democracy: Political control and the provision of Public Services. *Comparative Political Studies*, 34, 589-621.

10. Ibid.

11. Cremona, R.K. (2006). *A meaningful majority: Rediscovering government by the people*. Ph.D. Dissertation. State University of New York New York, United States, ATT 3220350.

12. Riker, W.H. (1993). Comments on Radcliff's "liberalism, populism and Collective Choice". *Political Research Quarterly,* Volume *46* (1). 143-149.

13. Asen, R. (2003). The Multiple Mr. Dewey: Multiple Publics and Permeable Borders in John Dewey's Theory of the Public Sphere. *Argumentation and Advocacy,* 39(3).

14. African Development Bank (2005). *African Development Report, 2005.*Oxford: Oxford University Press, p.197.

15. Diamond, L. (2008) *The Spirit of Democracy: The struggle to build free Societies throughout the World.* New York: Henry Holt.

16. United Nations (1966) International Covenant on Civil and Political Rights (ICCPR), United Nations General Assembly, New York.

17. Bertram, C. (2003). *Rousseau and the social Construct.* London: Routledge.

18. Kathi, P.C & Cooper, T.L. (2005). Democratizing the Administrative State: Connecting Neighborhood Councils and City Agencies. *Public Administration Review, 65*(5).

19. Roberts, N. (2004). Public Deliberation in an Age of Direct Citizen Participation. *American Review of Public Administration, 34* (4) pp.315-353.

20. Putnam, R. (2000). Bowling Alone: The Collapse and Revival of American Community. New York: Simon & Schuster.

21. Dahl, R. A. (1989). *Democracy and its critics.* New Haven, CT: Yale University Press.

22. Cooper, T. L. (1983). Citizen Participation. In *Organization Theory and Management*, edited by Thomas D. Lynch, 13-46. New York: Marcel Dekker.

23. Organski, A.F.K. (1973). The stages of political development. New York: Alfred A. Knopt.

24. Marshalls, M.G. & Jaggers, K. (2009) *Polity IV project: Political regime characteristics and transitions, 1800-2009.*Severn, MD: Center for systemic Peace.

25. Machiavelli, N. (1994). *The Prince.* Ed. Wooton, David. MA, Cambridge: Hackett Publishing.

26. Pettit, P. (1997). Republicanism: A theory of freedom and government. New York: Oxford Press.

27. Maynor, J. (2006). Modern republican democratic contestation: A model of deliberative democracy. In I. Honohan & J. Jennings, *Republicanism in Theory and practice, 125*-139. NY: Rout ledge, P.130.

28. Przeworski, A, Alvarez, M. Cheibub, J, & Limongi, F. (2000). *Democracy and Development: Political Institutions and Material Well-being in the World, 1950-1990.*Cambridge, MA: Cambridge Press.

29. Diamond, L. (2008) *The Spirit of Democracy: The struggle to build free Societies throughout the World.* New York: Henry Holt.

30. Dahl, R. A. (1989). *Democracy and its critics.* New Haven, CT: Yale University Press.

31. Cain, B.E. (1999). In Lipstz, K.L (2004). *Campaigns and Competition: How to Enhance Voter Knowledge and Deliberation in Mass Democracy.* Ph.D. Dissertation. University of California. Berkley, United States. AAT 3167206.

32. United Nations (1966) International Covenant on Civil and Political Rights, United Nations General Assembly, New York.

33. USAID Policy (1991). Democracy and Governance. Washington, DC.

Chapter 6: The Spectrum of Political Leadership: authoritarian to democratic Leadership

1. Fiedler, F. E. (1977). *Job engineering for effective leadership: A new approach. Management Review.* September Edition, p. 29.

2. Burns, J.M. (1978). *Leadership.* New York: Harper & Row.

3. Ibid.

4. McShane, S.L. & Von Glinov, M. A. (2005). *Organizational behavior.* New York: The McGraw-Hill Companies.

5. Ibid.

6. Ibid

7. Tannenbaum, R. & Schmidt, W.H. (1958). How to Choose a Leadership Pattern. *Harvard Business Review, 36*(2), 95-101.

8. Marshall, M.G & Cole, B.R. (2009). *Global report 2009.*Severn, MD: Center for systemic Peace.

9. Ibid.

10. Ibid, p.9).

11. Ibid.

12. Ekman, J. (2009). Political participation and regime stability: A framework for analyzing hybrid regimes. *International Political Science Review. 30* (1), 7-31.

13 Pepinsky, T. (2007). Durable authoritarianism as a self-enforcing coalition. Conference Paper, 2007 annual meeting of the American Political Science Association, Chicago, IL, p.3.

14. Gerring, J., Philip, B., Barndt, W. T. & Moreno, C. (2005). Democracy and economic growth: A historical perspective. *World Politics, 57*, 323-264.

15. Shafritz, J.M., Russell, E.W. & Borick, C.P. (2007). *Introducing Public Administration.*5[th]Ed.New York: Pearson-Longman.

16. Ibid.
17. Ibid.
18. Marshalls, M.G. & Jaggers, K. (2009) *Polity IV project: Political regime characteristics and transitions, 1800-2009*.Severn, MD: Center for systemic Peace.
19. Madueke, C.N. (2008). *The role of leadership in governance: The Nigerian experience*. Ph.D. Dissertation. Walden University. ATT3320296.
20. Ibid.
21. Shafritz, J.M., Russell, E.W. & Borick, C.P. (2007). *Introducing Public Administration* .5[th]Ed.New York: Pearson-Longman.
22. Marshall, M.G & Cole, B.R. (2009). *Global report 2009*.Severn, MD: Center for systemic Peace. P. 9
23. Ekman, J. (2009). Political participation and regime stability: A framework for analyzing hybrid regimes. *International Political Science Review. 30* (1), 7-31.
24. Ibid.

Chapter 7: Problems of Democratic Practices in Nigeria

1. Ekman, J. (2009). Political participation and regime stability: A framework for analyzing hybrid regimes. *International Political Science Review. 30* (1), 7-31.
2. Levitsky, S. & Way, L.A. (2009). *Competitive authoritarianism: The emergence and dynamics of hybrid regimes in the post-cold war era*. New York, NY: Cambridge University Press.
3. Diamond, L. (1999). *Developing Democracy: Towards Consolidation.* Baltimore, MD: Johns Hopkins Press, p. 3.
4. Shapiro, I. (2004). *The moral foundations of politics.* New Haven, CT: Yale University Press.
5. Diamond, L. (2008) *The Spirit of Democracy: The struggle to build free Societies throughout the World.* New York: Henry Holt and Company, p.155.
6. Ibid, p.167).
7Sandbrook, R. (1985). The Politics of Africa's Economic Stagnation. New York: Press Syndicate, Cambridge University Press., p. 46
8. Ibid, p.46.
9. Ibid, p.45.
10. Ibid, p.45.
11. Ibid
12. Rotberg, R. (2009). Governance and leadership in Africa: Measures, methods and results (Ibrahim index of African governance report). *Journal of International Affairs,* 62.
13. Diamond, L. (2008) *The Spirit of Democracy: The struggle to build free Societies throughout the World.* New York: Henry Holt.
14. Ibid.
15. Ibid, p.155).
16. Okoye, I. (2007). Political godfatherism, electoral politics and governance in Nigeria. Paper presented at the 65th Annual Conference of MPSA held in Chicago, USA, April 12-15, 2007, p.2.

17. Ikpe, U. B. (2009). The impact of manipulated re-elections on accountability and legitimacy of democratic regimes in Africa: Observations from Nigeria, Zambia and Kenya. *African Journal of Political Science and International Relations, 3(7),* pp. 300-310.

18. Ibid.

19. Ibid, p.301).

20. Ibid, p. 303).

21. Diamond, L. (2008) *The Spirit of Democracy: The struggle to build free Societies throughout the World.* New York: Henry Holt.

22. Marshall, M.G & Cole, B.R. (2009). *Global report 2009.*Severn, MD: Center for systemic Peace.

23. Ibid, p.9

24. Ibid, p.9

25. Ibid, p.9

26. Ibid.

27. Ibid, p.9

28. Ibid, p.9

29. Center for Systemic Peace (2014).www. Systemicpeace.org.

Chapter 8: Nigeria's Political Leadership Problems

1. Osinakachukwu, N.P., Jawan, J.A. & Redzuan, M. (2011). The success and shortcomings of democratic development in Nigeria from 1960 to 1999: An Overview. *Journal of Politics and Law, 4(1),* 166-174.

2. Alence, R. (2004). Political institutions and development governance in Sub-Saharan Africa. *Journal of Modern African Studies, 42* (2), 163-187.

3. Ibid.

4. Ibid.

5. Van de Walle, N. (2000).The Impact of Multiparty politics in Sub-Saharan Africa. Norwegian Association for development Research Annual Conference, Bergen, Norway.

6. Diamond, L. (2008) *The Spirit of Democracy: The struggle to build free Societies throughout the World.* New York: Henry Holt.

7. Ibid.

8. Wong, P.T.P. (2003.*An Opponent-process Model of Servant Leadership and a Typology of Leadership Styles.* Paper presented at the servant Leadership Roundtable at Regent University, Virginia Beach, VA, on October, 16, 2003.

9. Ames, B. (1987). Political Survival: Politicians and public policy in Latin America, Berkley, CA.

10. USAID Policy (1991). Democracy and Governance. Washington, DC

11. Osinakachukwu, N.P., Jawan, J.A. & Redzuan, M. (2011). The success and shortcomings of democratic development in Nigeria from 1960 to 1999: An Overview. *Journal of Politics and Law, 4(1),* 166-174.

12. Ikpe, U. B. (2009). The impact of manipulated re-elections on accountability and legitimacy of democratic regimes in Africa: Observations from Nigeria, Zambia and Kenya. *African Journal of Political Science and International*

Relations, 3(7), pp. 300-310, p. 303.
13. Alence, R. (2004). Political institutions and development governance in Sub-Saharan Africa. *Journal of Modern African Studies, 42* (2), 163-187.
14. Transparency International (2010). *Corruption perception index*. Berlin: Transparency International.
15. Rotberg, R. (2004). Strengthening Africa leadership. *Foreign Affairs, 83* (4), 14-18.
16. Ibid.
17. Obama, B.H.(2006).An honest Government-A hopeful future. Speech delivered at the University of Nairobi, Kenya, on August 8[th]2006.
18. Kaufmann, D., Kraay, A; & Mastruzzi, M. (2009). Governance matters VIII: Aggregate   and individual governance indicators, 2008. *World Bank Policy Research Working Paper* No. 4978, Washington, DC.
19. Ibid.
20. Ibid.
21. Mo Ibrahim Foundation (2010). *2010 Ibrahim index of African governance: Summary*. http://www.moibrahimfoundation.org/.

Chapter 9: Nigeria: A Predatory Political System?

1. Diamond, L. (2008) *The Spirit of Democracy: The struggle to build free Societies throughout the World.* New York: Henry Holt.
2. Ibid
3. Ibid, p.298
4. Ibid.
5. Ibid, p.298
6. Sandbrook (1985). The Politics of Africa's Economic Stagnation. New York: Press Syndicate, Cambridge University Press, p. 67.
7. Diamond, L. (2008) *The Spirit of Democracy: The struggle to build free Societies Throughout the World.* New York: Henry Holt, p.298.
8. Ibid.
9. Ibid, p.298
10. Ibid, p.298
11. Ibid.
12. Ibid, p.299
13. Sandbrook, R. (1985) The Politics of Africa's Economic Stagnation. New York: Press Syndicate, Cambridge University Press
14. Diamond, L. (2008) *The Spirit of Democracy: The struggle to build free Societies throughout the World.* New York: Henry Holt.
15. Ibid.

Chapter 10: Political Problems Affecting National Development

1. Brinkman, R.L. (1995). Economic Growth versus Economic Development: Towards a Conceptual Clarification. *Journal of Economic Issues*, Volume 29(4), pp.1171-1188.
2. Frietzgerald, M, (1989). A new View of Economic Growth. New York: Oxford

University Press.

3. Breese, G.(1966). Urbanization in Newly Developing Countries, Englewood Cliffs, New Jersey: Prentice-Hall.

4. Organski, A.F.K. (1973). The stages of political development. New York: Alfred A. Knopt.

5. Schraeder, P.J. (2004). *African politics and society: A mosaic in transformation.* New York: Thomson Belmont.

6. Bratton, M. & Mattes, R.(2001).Africa's Surprising Universalism. Journal of Democracy, Volume 12(1).

7. Yuan, P. (2009). Modernization theory. *Chinese studies in history*, 43(1), 37-45.

8. Hosseini, H.(2003).Why Development is more complex Than Growth: clarifying some confusions. *Review of social economy*, LXI (1),pp.93-110.

9. Ibid.

10. World Bank (1992). *World Development Report.* New York: Oxford Press.

11. USAID Policy (1991). Democracy and Governance. Washington, DC.

12. Kulger, J. & Feng, Y.(1999) Explaining and Modeling Democratic Transitions. The Journal of Conflicts Resolution, 43(2), pp.139-147.

13. Lipset, S. M. (1963). *Political Man: The social bases of politics.* Garden City, NY: Double day & Company.

14. Mozaffar, S. (2005). Negotiating Independence in Mauritius. *International Negotiation, 10*(2), 263–291.

15. ViewsWire, Nigeria (2010). *Risk briefing: Nigeria.* Country Profiles and Economic Data Web site.

16. Davis, J.H. & Ruhe, J.A. (2003) Perception of country corruption: antecedents and outcomes. *Journal of Business Ethics,* Volume 43(4), pp.275

17. Smith, D. J. (2010). Corruption, NGOs, and development in Nigeria. *Third World* Quarterly, 31(2), 243-258.

18. Mosley, P.(2004) Institutions and Politics in A Lewis-Type Growth Model. *The Manchester School*, Volume 72(6).

19. Ibid.

20. Diamond, L. (2008) *The Spirit of Democracy: The struggle to build free Societies throughout the World.* New York: Henry Holt, p.155.

21. Gerring, J., Philip, B., Barndt, W. T. & Moreno, C. (2005). Democracy and economic growth: A historical perspective. *World Politics, 57*, 323-264, p.333.

22. Rotberg, R. (2007). *Governance and leadership in Africa*, Broomal, PA: Mason Crest Publishers.

23. Gerring, J., Philip, B., Barndt, W. T. & Moreno, C. (2005). Democracy and economic growth: A historical perspective. *World Politics, 57*, 323-264.

24. Alence, R. (2004). Political institutions and development governance in Sub-Saharan Africa. *Journal of Modern African Studies, 42* (2), 163-187.

25. Ibid.

26. Diamond, L. (2008) *The Spirit of Democracy: The struggle to build free Societies throughout the World.* New York: Henry Holt.

27. Ibid.

28. African Development Bank (2005). Public Sector Management in Africa. African Development Report 2005. New York: Oxford University Press
29. Ibid.
30. Ibid.
31. Ibid.
32. Casson, M., Giusta, D. & Kambhampati, U.S. (2010). Formal and informal and development. *World Development, 38*(2), 137-141.
33. Hernando De Soto (2001, p.11). The mystery of capital: Why capitalism triumphs in the West and fails everywhere else. New York: Basic Books.
34. World Bank (2003). Sustainable Development in a Dynamic World. *World Development Report*. New York: Oxford Press.
35. Wibbels, E. (2009). Cores, peripheries, and contemporary Political Economy. *St Comp .Int. Dev.*. Volume 44.pp441-449
36. Ibid.
37.UNDP (2014). United Nations Development Program, Human Development Report 2014. New York: Oxford Press.
38. UNDP (1994). United Nations Development Program, *Human Development Report*. New York: Oxford Press.
39. UNDP (2014). United Nations Development Program, Human Development Report 2014. New York: Oxford Press.
40. Ibid.
41-Imoh, C. (2012). The Relationship of Electoral Competition and presidential leadership performance: The case of Nigeria. Ph.D. Dissertation. ProQuest Dissertation & Thesis: Full Text Database ((Order Number UMI 3543356).

Chapter 11: Elections and Political Leadership Performance
1. Rotberg, R. (2009). Governance and leadership in Africa: Measures, methods and results. *Journal of International Affairs,* 62.
2. Maynor, J. (2006). Modern republican democratic contestation: A model of deliberative democracy. In I. Honohan & J. Jennings, *Republicanism in Theory and practice, 125*-139. NY: Rout ledge.
3. Tvinnereim, E. M. (2004). *Democratic contestation, accountability and citizen satisfaction in German states.* Paper presented at the annual Meeting of The Midwest Political Science Association, Palmar House Hilton, Chicago, Illinois.
4. Ikpe, U. B. (2009). The impact of manipulated re-elections on accountability and legitimacy of democratic regimes in Africa: Observations from Nigeria, Zambia and Kenya. *African Journal of Political Science and International Relations, 3(7),* pp. 300-310.
5. Dahl, R. A. (1971). *Polyarchy.* New Haven, CT: Yale University Press, p.39.
6. USAID Policy (1991). Democracy and Governance. Washington, DC.
7. LeVan, A. (2007). *Dictators, democrats and development in Nigeria. A PhD Dissertation,* University of California, San Diego. AAT 3283913.
8. Ibid.
9. Tvinnereim, E. M. (2004). *Democratic contestation, accountability and citizen satisfaction in German states.* Paper presented at the annual Meeting of The

Midwest Political Science Association, Palmar House Hilton, Chicago, Illinois.
10. Chan, S. (1997). Democracy and Inequality: Tracing welfare spending in Singapore, Taiwan, and South Korea. In Inequality, democracy, and economic Development. Ed. Midlarsky, M. I. Cambridge: Cambridge University Press.
11. Beer, C. & Mitchell, N.J. (2004). Democracy and human rights in the Mexican state: Elections or Social Capital? *International Studies Quarterly*, *48*, 293-312.
12. Rakner, L. & van de Walle, N. (2009). Democratization by elections? Opposition weakness in Africa. *Journal of Democracy, 20(3),* 108-258.

Chapter 12: Political Leadership performance and Development
1. Brinkman, R.L. (1995). Economic Growth versus Economic Development: Towards a Conceptual Clarification. *Journal of Economic Issues*, Volume 29 (4), pp.1171-1188.
 2. Jennings, A. & Waller, W. (1994).Evolutionary Economics and cultural Hermeneutics: Veblen, Cultural relativism, blind drift. *Journal of Economics,* 28(4), pp.997-1030.
3. USAID Policy (1991). Democracy and Governance. Washington, DC
4. Ibid.

Chapter 13: Elections, Leadership, and National Development
1. Boix, C. (2003). Democracy and Redistribution. Cambridge, MA; Cambridge University Press.
2. Schultz, P.T (1999).Health and Schooling Investment in Africa. Journal of Economic Perspectives, 13(3), pp.67-88.
3. Basu, A. & Srinivasan, K. (2002) Foreign Direct Investment in Africa. *IMF Working Paper*, WP/02/61.
4. Lipset, S. M. (1963). *Political Man: The social bases of politics.* Garden City, NY: Double day & Company.
5. Ibid, p.71.
6. Ibid, p.72.
7. Boix, C. (2003). Democracy and Redistribution. Cambridge, MA; Cambridge University Press.
8. Landman, T. (1999, p.607). Economic Development and Democracy: The view from Latin America, *Political Studies, XLVII.*
9. Kulger, J. & Feng, Y. (1999) Explaining and Modeling Democratic Transitions. The Journal of Conflicts Resolution, 43(2), pp.139-147.
10. Lipset, S. M. (1959). Some Social requisites of democracy: Economic development and political Legitimacy. Bobbs-Merrill.
11. Mozaffar, S. (2005). Negotiating Independence in Mauritius. *International Negotiation, 10*(2), 263–291, p. 264.
12. Gerring, J., Philip, B., Barndt, W. T. & Moreno, C. (2005). Democracy and economic growth: A historical perspective. *World Politics, 57*, 323-264, p. 333.

Chapter 14: Assessing Electoral Competition in Nigeria
1. Marshalls, M.G. & Jaggers, K. (2009) *Polity IV project: Political regime*

*characteristics and transitions, 1800-2009.*Severn, MD: Center for systemic Peace.

2. Rotberg, R. (2007). *Governance and leadership in Africa*, Broomal, PA: Mason Crest Publishers.

3. Ibid.

4. Ibid.

5. Satyanath, S. & Subramanian, A. (2004). What determines long-run macroeconomic stability? *IMF Working paper No 04/215.*

6. Shapiro, I. (2004). *The moral foundations of politics.* New Haven, CT: Yale University Press.

7. Rosenstone, S.J., Behr, R. & Lazarus, E.H. (1984). *Third Parties in America: Citizen Response to Major Party Failure.* Princeton: Princeton University Press, p.222.

8. Marshalls, M.G. & Jaggers, K. (2009) *Polity IV project: Political regime characteristics and transitions, 1800-2009.*Severn, MD: Center for systemic Peace.

9. Lipset, S. M. (1963). *Political Man: The social bases of politics.* Garden City, NY: Double day & Company.

10. Tvinnereim, E. M. (2004). *Democratic contestation, accountability and citizen satisfaction in German states.* Paper presented at the annual Meeting of The Midwest Political Science Association, Palmar House Hilton, Chicago, Illinois.

11. LeVan, A. (2007). *Dictators, democrats and development in Nigeria. A PhD Dissertation,* University of California, San Diego. AAT 3283913.

12. Tvinnereim, E. M. (2004). *Democratic contestation, accountability and citizen satisfaction in German states.* Paper presented at the annual Meeting of The Midwest Political Science Association, Palmar House Hilton, Chicago, Illinois.

13. Satyanath, S. & Subramanian, A. (2004). What determines long-run macroeconomic stability? *IMF Working paper No 04/215.*

14. Marshall, M.G & Cole, B.R. (2009). *Global report 2009.*Severn, MD: Center for systemic Peace.

15. Gurr, T.R. Jaggers, K. & Moore, W. (1990). The transformation of Western state: Indicators of democracy, autocracy, and state power since 1800. *Studies in Comparative International Development, 25*(1), 73-108.

16. Marshall, M.G & Cole, B.R. (2009). *Global report 2009.*Severn, MD: Center for systemic Peace.

17. Ibid.

18. Coa, F. (2009). Modernization theory and China's road to modernization. *Chinese Studies in History, 43*(1), p.8.

19. International IDEA (2008). *Assessing the quality of democracy: An overview of the international IDEA framework.* Stockholm: International IDEA.

20. Ibid.

Chapter 15: Assessing Presidential Leadership Performance in Nigeria

1. Zaleznik, A. (2004). Managers and leaders: Are they different? *Harvard Business* Review (Reprint), *82*(1), 74-82.
2. Yukl, G. (2006). *Leadership in organizations.* 6th Ed. Upper Saddle River, NJ: Prentice Hall.
3. Kaufmann, D., Kraay, A; & Mastuzzi, M. (2009, p.6). Governance matters VIII: Aggregate and individual governance indicators, 2008. *World Bank Policy Research Working Paper* No. 4978, Washington, DC.
4. Rotberg, R. (2007). *Governance and leadership in Africa*, Broomal, PA: Mason Crest Publishers.
5. Ibid.
6. Mo Ibrahim Foundation (2010). *2010 Ibrahim index of African governance: Summary.* http://www.moibrahimfoundation.org/
7. Rotberg, R. (2009). Governance and leadership in Africa: Measures, methods and results (Ibrahim index of African governance report). *Journal of International Affairs,* 62.
8. International IDEA (2008). *Assessing the quality of democracy: An overview of the international IDEA framework.* Stockholm: International IDEA.
9. Rotberg, R. (2007). *Governance and leadership in Africa*, Broomal, PA: Mason Crest Publishers.
10. Ibid.
11. Ibid.
12. Gerring, J., Philip, B., Barndt, W. T. & Moreno, C. (2005). Democracy and economic growth: A historical perspective. *World Politics, 57*, 323-264.
13. ViewsWire, Nigeria (2010). *Risk briefing: Nigeria.* Country Profiles and Economic Data Web site.
14. (Riker, 1993)
15. (Rotberg, 2007). Rotberg, R. (2007). *Governance and leadership in Africa*, Broomal, PA: Mason Crest Publishers.
16. Ojo, E.O. (2006). Human rights and sustainable democracy in Nigeria (1999-2003). Journal of Social Science, *13*(1), 15-29.
17. Rotberg, R. (2007). *Governance and leadership in Africa*, Broomal, PA: Mason Crest Publishers.
18. USAID Policy (1991). Democracy and Governance. Washington, DC
19. Imoh, C. (2012). The Relationship of Electoral Competition and presidential leadership performance: The case of Nigeria. Ph.D. Dissertation. ProQuest Dissertation & Thesis: Full Text Database ((Order Number UMI 3543356).
20. Davis, J.H. & Ruhe, J.A. (2003) Perception of country corruption: antecedents and outcomes. *Journal of Business Ethics,* Volume 43(4).
21. Ibid.
22. ViewsWire, Nigeria (2010). *Risk briefing: Nigeria.* Country Profiles and Economic Data Web site.
23. Greenwood, D., Daphne, T. & Holt, R. (2008). Institutional and ecological economics: The role of technology and institution in economic development. *Journal of Economic Issues, 42* (2), 445-450.
24. Coa, F. (2009). Modernization theory and China's road to modernization.

Chinese Studies in History, 43(1).
25. Ibid.
26. Yuan, P. (2009). Modernization theory. *Chinese studies in history, 43*(1), 37-45.
27. UNDP (2010). United Nations Development Program, *Human development report, 2010*. New York, NY: Oxford Press.

Chapter 16: Electoral competition and Presidential Leadership Performance: Research Study on Nigeria

1. Imoh, c. (2012). The Relationship of Electoral Competition and presidential leadership performance: The case of Nigeria. Ph.D. Dissertation. ProQuest Dissertation & Thesis: Full Text Database ((Order Number UMI 3543356).
2. Ibid.
3. Armijo, L.E. (2001). *Financial Globalization and Democracy in Emerging Markets*. New York: Palgrave.
4. Ibid.
5. Carothers, T. (2002). The end of the transition paradigm. Journal of Democracy, 13(1).
6. Ibid.
7. Maynor, J. (2006). Modern republican democratic contestation: A model of deliberative democracy. In I. Honohan & J. Jennings, *Republicanism in Theory and practice, 125*-139. NY: Rout ledge.
8. Huntington, S.P. (1993). The Third Wave: Democratization in the Late 20th Century. Norman, OK: University of Oklahoma Press.

Chapter 17: Enthronement of Genuine Electoral Competition

1. Dahl, R. A. (1971). *Polyarchy.* New Haven, CT: Yale University Press.
2. USAID Policy (1991). Democracy and Governance. Washington, DC.
3. Maynor, J. (2006). Modern republican democratic contestation: A model of deliberative democracy. In I. Honohan & J. Jennings, *Republicanism in Theory and practice, 125*-139. NY: Rout ledge.
4. Foweraker, J. & Krznaric, R. (2001). How to construct a database of liberal democratic performance. *Democratization, 8*(3), 1-25.
5. Maynor, J. (2006). Modern republican democratic contestation: A model of deliberative democracy. In I. Honohan & J. Jennings, *Republicanism in Theory and practice, 125*-139. NY: Rout ledge.
6. Mylonas, H. & Roussias, N. (2007). When do votes count? Regime type, electoral conduct and political competition in Africa. *Comparative Political Studies, 41(11),* 1466-1491, p. 1470.
7. Kang, M. (2008). Race and democratic contestation. *Yale Law Journal.* 117(734).
8. Ibid.
9. Ibid.

Chapter 18: Enthronement of Developmental Leadership

1. Bass, B.M. (1985). *Leadership and performance beyond expectations*. New York, NY: Free Press.
2. Burns, J.M. (1978). *Leadership*. New York: Harper & Row
3. Ibid.
4. McShane, S.L. & Von Glinov, M. A. (2005). *Organizational behavior*. New York: The McGraw-Hill Companies.
5. Trevion, L.K., Brown, M. & Hartman, L.P. (2003). A qualitative investigation of perceived Executive Ethical Leadership: Perceptions from Inside and Outside the Executive Suite. *Human Relations.* Volume *56*(1), pp.5-28.
6. Ibid.
7. Larson, C.E. & LaFasto, F.M.(1989).*Teamwork.* Newbury Park, CA: Sage
8. Kotter, J. (1990). *A force for Change. How Leadership Differs From Management*. New York: Guilford Press.
9. McShane, S.L. & Von Glinov, M. A. (2005). *Organizational behavior*. New York: The McGraw-Hill Companies, p. 421.
10. Ibid.
11. House, R.J. & Mitchell, T.R. (1974) Path-Goal Theory of Leadership. *Journal of Contemporary Business,* Autumn Edition, pp.81-97.
12. Fiedler, F. E. (1977). *Job engineering for effective leadership: A new approach. Management Review*. September Edition, p. 29.
13. Van Wart, M. & Dicke, L.A. (2008). *Administrative leadership in the public sector.* Armonk, NY: M.E.Sharpe.
14. Fiedler, F. E. (1977). *Job engineering for effective leadership: A new approach. Management Review*. September Edition, p.10).

Chapter 19: Curbing corruption: The Curse of National Development

1. Quah, J.S. (2003). Curbing Corruption in Asia. Singapore: Eastern Universities.
2. Gberevbie, D.E. (2009). Democracy and the future of the Nigerian State. *Journal of Social Development in Africa, 24*(1), 165-191, p. 172.
3. Diamond, L. (2008). *The Spirit of Democracy: The struggle to build free Societies throughout the World.* New York: Henry Holt.

Chapter 20: Prospects for Exemplary Leadership

1. Alence, R. (2004). Political institutions and development governance in Sub-Saharan Africa. *Journal of Modern African Studies, 42* (2), 163-187.
2. Lo, S.S.H.(2006). Ethical Governance and Anti-Corruption in Greater China: A Comparison of Mainland China, Hong Kong and Macao. CPSA/ACSP papers. Htt://:www.cpsa-acsp.ca/papers-2006/Lo.pdf.
3. African Development Bank (2005). African Development Report (2005). Public Sector Management in Africa. New York: Oxford University Press.
4. Rotberg, R. (2004). Strengthening Africa leadership. *Foreign Affairs, 83* (4), 14-18.
5. Ibid.
6. Ibid.